Conflict
Resolution

Conflict Resolution

Vivian Einstein Gordon J.D., Ph.D.

WEST PUBLISHING COMPANY
St. Paul, New York, Los Angeles, San Francisco

Copyediting: Kathleen Pruno
Illustrations: Jim Kiehne

COPYRIGHT © 1988 By WEST PUBLISHING COMPANY
      50 W. Kellogg Boulevard
      P.O. Box 64526
      St. Paul, MN 55164–1003

Library of Congress Cataloging-in-Publication Data

Einstein Gordon, Vivian.
  Conflict resolution.

  Bibliography: p.
  1. Conflict management. I. Title.
HD42.E34 1988   658.4 85–51392
ISBN 0–314–62318–3

To my family with love: to my outstanding children, Douglas, Mark, and Richard and to my wonderful husband, Michael.

Contents

Preface

Legal theorists and members of the legal profession readily admit that negotiation, mediation and arbitration are used to resolve legal disputes in addition to and as alternatives to trial. Conservative research indicates that less than 10% of all cases filed ever go to trial in state or federal courts. This number does not include those legal cases which are settled by lawyers before cases are filed, nor does it include all the legal disputes where individuals decide not to spend the time, money and effort to see a lawyer. The purpose of this book is to introduce negotiation, mediation and arbitration in addition to trials as means for resolving disputes. Though the initial concept of the book is to describe these processes in the context of legal disputes, the same processes are applicable to most disputes including but not limited to interpersonal, employment, corporate, community and global disputes. Concepts learned in *Conflict Resolution* will provide skills students can call upon in countless situations throughout their lives.

In conflict resolution, parties are on opposing sides of the same issue as compared to problem solving, where parties are concerned with how to solve a problem though they may have inherently different reasons for wanting the problem solved. The distinction between conflict resolution and problem solving is made only initially with the notion that though the distinction exists, the processes used to deal with each are similar.

The book has been divided into three major areas: negotiation, mediation and arbitration. Chapter 1 is introductory, indicating how legal disputes are resolved through the litigation process, up to and including trials, with emphasis on how dispute resolution processes are used by lawyers and the legal system.

Chapter 2 begins a series of chapters on negotiation which is one of the major processes used in resolving legal and other disputes. This chapter examines the steps in the process of negotiation, introduces conflict exercises and offers a negotiation plan. Chapter 3 details possible methods and approaches negotiators take, noting that multiple methods and approaches are often used during the course of negotiation. Chapter 4 highlights pervasive obstacles that get in the way of resolving disputes; Chapter 5 examines methods for overcoming them. Chapter 6 is a review of conflicts presented in children's literature. The application of learned negotiation concepts to this array of stories can lead to fascinating class discussion.

Chapters 7 and 8 cover mediation. Chapter 7 examines the steps in the process of mediation, while Chapter 8 details these steps and their application to critical issues.

Chapters 9 and 10 are devoted to arbitration. Chapter 9 provides a skeletal view and Chapter 10 presents details of the process and some sample problems.

Critical attention has been given to the development of the problems offered within the context of each dispute resolution process. They begin with simple interpersonal disputes, school disputes, and individual versus company disputes, and move toward individual versus community disputes, landlord versus tenant disputes, employee versus employer disputes, corporate disputes, community disputes and global disputes. This design is intended to provide the reader with the understanding that the same steps used in handling simple interpersonal disputes are used in handling complex disputes. The variety of topics is intended to provide the reader with the awareness that knowledge of these processes brings power to handle a variety of disputes in everyday life, in the legal system and in the society in which we live.

Conflict Resolution can be presented as a segment within the social studies curriculum, but is also suitable for English and communication courses.

This book comes with a Teacher's Resource and Implementation Manual. The manual supplements the book with activities, problems and reading materials. The implementation material is designed to guide school districts in implementing such a program in their school systems.

Acknowledgments

The book has gone through extensive two year traditional piloting in the Chicago Public Schools through the cooperation of George Munoz, past president and member of the Chicago Board of Education; Dr. Manford Byrd, general superintendent of schools; Dr. Margaret Harrigan, associate superintendant; and Dr. Alice Jurica, director, Bureau of Social Studies. Such an effort would not have been possible without the efforts of these individuals and the wonderful teachers and students in the Chicago Public School System.

To outstanding men whose talents are legendary in the field of conflict resolution and who gave their time and efforts to this project, my never ending thanks: Professor Frank Sander, Harvard Law School; Professor Stephen Goldberg, Northwestern Law School; Duane M. Buckmaster, deputy director, Federal Mediation and Conciliation Service; William Hartgering, Endispute; Richard

Salem, Loyola University School of Law, Samuel T. Lawton, Jr., Altheimer and Gray; Herb Cohen, author, teacher, negotiator for nations. These men served much as an advisory panel might, providing their continued expertise and valued wisdom.

Several other teachers evaluated this book during its development and provided extremely helpful suggestions:

Dorothy Cutlip
Barrington High School
Barrington, Illinois

Jacqueline Cyrus
Washington D.C. Public
Schools
Silver Spring, Maryland

Carol D. Fanning
Marshfield School System
Scituate, Massachusetts

Rita Hendershot
Gonzales Independent
School District
Gonzales, Texas

Judith M. Johnson
Ellenville Central School
Ellenville, New York

Emily S. Jonas
Philadelphia, Pennsylvania

Charlene G. Meyer
Monterey School
Colorado Springs, Colorado

Dorothie C. Shah
Evanston Township High
School
Evanston, Illinois

Nan D. Stein, Ed.D.
Massachusetts Department
of Education
Arlington, Massachusetts

Support for the development of this book and the Conflict Resolution Program came from three major sources. Though dispute resolution has grown substantially over the last few years, when this book and program were embryonic, it took the great vision of these institutions and their representatives for this work to go forward. West Publishing Company provided assistance during the development and piloting of *Conflict Resolution.* Teacher training costs have been funded by the American Bar Association-Law Student Division. The John Marshall Law School, in its continuing effort to provide public programs on the law, has spearheaded this effort.

It is my hope that students not only learn these concepts which, I believe, are fundamental to individuals' interactions within society, but also that they have some fun doing so.

Dr. Vivian Einstein Gordon

About the Author

Dr. Vivian Einstein Gordon is a lawyer, a law professor and has a Ph.D. in Administration and Public Policy. For two years she served as a research fellow at the University of Chicago Law School, Center for Criminal Justice. She has received numerous awards including Outstanding Young Woman Lawyer of the Year Award, 1983; Outstanding Young Woman of America, 1983; United Nations International Youth Year Award, 1985; National Bar Association Award, 1985; and she is listed in the 1987 *Who's Who in the Midwest.*

In 1986 she was one of twelve law professors nationally to win a fellowship from the National Endowment for the Humanities Bicentennial for the Constitution. In addition to practicing law she has served as a grant reviewer for the U.S. Office of Education, as a consultant for the Illinois Board of Education, and as a member of the North Central Accreditation Committee and the Chicago Community School Study Commission. She is a certified arbitrator with the American Arbitration Association and has served as director for a number of law-related education programs which she initiated, developed and implemented. She has authored numerous articles, has lectured extensively, and has appeared on radio and television programs as an expert in legal conflict resolution, school law, and juvenile law.

Conflict
Resolution

PART I

Negotiation

CHAPTER 1

Negotiation, Mediation, Arbitration, and the Legal System

Most people think legal cases are settled in a trial. In fact, most legal cases are settled by negotiation, mediation, and arbitration. Research indicates that over 90 percent of all cases in state and federal courts throughout the United States are settled before they go to trial. This research does not consider all the legal cases not filed but settled quietly by lawyers; the research also doesn't include all legal cases for which people decide, for many reasons, not to go to a lawyer. Thus only a small percent of all legal cases are actually settled by a trial.

If this is true, how are legal cases *really settled?* The litigation process is sometimes described like this:

First, a legal case is **filed** in a court. Then a period of **discovery** follows, during which the lawyer collects evidence and testimony not only from the client, but also from all other individuals who may know about the case.

Pretrial motions are argued and **pretrial conferences** are held during this period. Pretrial motions are preliminary issues argued by lawyers in court and decided by the judge. Pretrial conferences are meetings held before trial where the judge and the lawyers resolve some issues and decide which issues go to trial. Prior to a *jury trial,* lawyers go through **voir dire,** the process used to choose jurors in a jury trial. In jury trials, jurors are the fact-finders. In *bench trials,* judges are the fact-finders. Finally, a **trial** on the remaining issues is held.

Thus, the litigation process includes filing the case, discovery of evidence and testimony, pretrial motions and pretrial conferences, voir dire in jury trials, and the trial.

In reality, however, many legal cases never get filed or go to trial. What really happens in a legal case is something like this:

Stage 1

A client goes to a lawyer with a problem and asks for help. The lawyer will ask questions about the facts of the case and will counsel the client on the law about the legal issues. The lawyer will describe generally what happens to a legal case in the litigation process, and will also describe the strengths and weaknesses of this client's case. The lawyer may even indicate the client's probable chances of winning the case in a trial.

If the client has little or no chance of winning, the lawyer may suggest not going to trial or even filing a lawsuit. The lawyer may suggest, however, that rather than dropping the entire case, a meeting be set up with the other individual in the dispute. At this **negotiation** meeting, the lawyer would try to see if something can be resolved to the client's satisfaction.

If the client has some chance or a probable chance of winning, the lawyer may suggest filing a lawsuit *and* may also suggest setting up a meeting to discuss the problem with the other party. This use of negotiation may result in a faster settlement than waiting to go to trial. It may also save both parties the cost of collecting evidence and testimony. Saving costs and time are often reasons for negotiation of a legal dispute, even a winning case.

Therefore, in Stage 1 of a legal case, many winning *and* losing cases are settled by negotiation before a lawsuit is ever filed in court.

Stage 2

If the case is filed in court, the lawyer then proceeds with the **discovery** phase. During this phase, the lawyer collects testimony and evidence. Depositions are taken from the client, the opposing party and all other individuals related to the case. **Depositions** are statements made during an interview with the lawyers that are recorded. **Interrogatories** may be sent; these are written questions to be answered by the parties involved in the dispute. **Evidence** is also collected.

In this discovery phase of the litigation process facts or statements may come up that weaken the client's case or become obstacles in winning the case: witnesses may not be as positive about seeing or hearing things as first thought; evidence may be found that contradicts the client's story; other witnesses may indicate different facts. Many events occur during discovery that may point out to the lawyer the weaknesses of the case.

The lawyer may often apprise the client of the evidence and testimony as it unfolds, including weaknesses and difficulties that arise. At this stage, the lawyer may suggest negotiation with the other attorney to discuss how the case may be settled prior to trial. The lawyer may describe to the client the strengths and weaknesses of the case and indicate that at trial, one person wins and one person loses. Because of this risk, the client's best interests may be served by settling the case prior to trial.

Therefore, in Stage 2 of a legal case, the weaknesses and strengths of a case may be taken into consideration for earlier settlement through negotiation.

Stage 3

Many preliminary legal issues or **pretrial motions** must be decided by a judge during the litigation process. These preliminary motions are brought to court during discovery. As in a trial, one party wins and one party loses these motions. The lawyer whose motion loses may, at that time, indicate to the client that this may be a good time to try to negotiate and settle the case before trial. The lawyer may even suggest bringing the case before an **arbitrator** for an **arbitration.** This is a private hearing of the case where a decision is made by a third person, or arbitrator, chosen by the parties in the dispute. The result is binding and enforceable in a court of law. An arbitration is fast and lacks the formalities of a courtroom trial.

Even if some pretrial motions are won or lost and the client proceeds to go forward with a trial, prior to trial is generally a **pretrial conference.** The lawyers and the judge attend this conference. Some issues are settled through discussion and negotiation at this time. Sometimes the judge takes an active role in **mediating** and encouraging the lawyers to settle cases here, particularly when the judge believes that the parties' best interests are served by not going to trial, or when the issues are such that they can be settled without a trial.

Therefore, in Stage 3 of a legal case, pretrial motions or discussions during pretrial conferences may lead to a negotiated resolution of the legal dispute.

Stage 4

Though a case may have gone through all the prior stages of the litigation process, even during **voir dire,** when a jury is being selected and right up to the time of trial, cases are often settled. This occurs for a number of reasons. Perhaps some of the witnesses have trouble coming to court; perhaps new evidence has surfaced; perhaps the case does not appear to be as strong as first thought; perhaps some of the witnesses may not be effective during questioning; perhaps the cost of a trial is prohibitive; perhaps time has become an issue and one party has to settle quickly.

Whatever the reason, cases are often negotiated before trial in Stage 4.

Stage 5

Trial is a process where both parties put forward their best case and the fact finder, whether it is a judge or a jury, decides who wins and who loses. Winners, of course, are pleased. Losers may say they are pleased to have had their "day in court," but as they think about it, they may become less pleased. They may begin to question the legal system, their lawyer, the witnesses, the judge, or the jury. They may refuse to do what the court ordered because they are angry about losing. They may even leave town. Thus, the winners, though they may win the trial, may not get what was decided.

Research indicates that people are more likely to perform an agreement if they have participated in its creation and are active participants in its formulation. They are also more likely to carry out an agreement if they feel they will get something out of it and are not the total losers in the outcome of the dispute. If this research is correct, then a trial where the parties do not decide the outcome and where one party loses is a process that may not encourage performance or action on the agreement or court decision.

For example, in a divorce one parent may have legal custody of the child, but both parents must continue to support and care for the child, must see and visit the child, and must be involved in the child's growth and development. Researchers suggest **mediation** is a more appropriate process than trial for these issues. This is because in mediation the parties themselves must make the agreement. The parents will have an ongoing relationship with the child, and they must continue to perform their part of the agreement for the sake of the child. A trial and its win-lose outcome is not as conducive for settling this issue as mediation, where both parties create the agreement that is just right for them. A win-win outcome allows both parties to feel that they won something in the dispute.

Therefore, in Stage 5, even if there is a trial, the win-lose outcome of trial does not guarantee that the parties will perform on the judgment. In some cases other conflict resolution processes that produce a win-win outcome to the dispute are preferable because the parties are more likely to perform on the agreement.

Sometimes mediation and arbitration are processes already decided in advance to be used when disputes arise. For example, many employment contracts state that arbitration will be used to solve any employee grievances. Thus, when employees are hired and sign the contract, they agree to arbitration. When negotiation, mediation and arbitration are stipulated between the parties, they are used instead of trials. Thus, negotiation, mediation, and arbitration in addition to trials are the processes used in settling legal cases.

Plea Bargaining in Criminal Cases: Negotiation

In criminal law, when an individual is accused of a crime the parties in the dispute are not the perpetrator and the victim. The parties are the perpetrator and the government. The reason is that for some human behavior, our society has created laws and penalties for its own protection and wants to protect all citizens from such antisocial actions. These laws are criminal laws and are listed in the state or federal criminal code.

When individuals are arrested and charged with a crime, or violation of the criminal law, they may be accused of a variety of crimes. The government wants to make sure all possible crimes are listed though the variety of charges may ultimately not be proven in trial. As evidence and testimony arise during discovery, and pretrial motions are made, the weaknesses and strengths in the case may surface. The lawyer representing the state may feel that enough evidence is available to convict the defendant. Or the state's attorney may find weaknesses in the state's case. The defendant's attorney may feel that the client's case has weaknesses and strengths. At that time, the state's attorney or the defendant's lawyer with approval of the client may suggest **plea bargaining,** which is the admission of guilt of a crime clearly committed in exchange for no trial and perhaps a lesser penalty. This is a form of negotiation between the state and the criminal defendant. The state is concerned that trials are time consuming, costly, and public. Plea bargaining is fast, less costly, and private. The defendant may agree, given the nature of the case, to have the lawyer participate in *plea* bargaining where the defendant will *plead* guilty rather than innocent to a charge and perhaps receive a lesser sentence.

Thus, even in criminal law, negotiation and settlement may occur without a trial. This, too, is considered legitimate alternative dispute resolution.

Conclusion

Most legal cases are settled before they go to trial. The processes used to settle these cases are negotiation, mediation, and arbitration. These processes are called alternative dispute resolution or ADR.

A number of factors encourage settlement rather than trial: costs of the litigation process; time needed to complete a case and go to trial; risk of losing the case; possibility of either party not performing his or her part of the court decision.

Lawyers take many factors into consideration when suggesting ADR: evidence that arises during discovery, the outcome of pretrial motions and pretrial conferences, risks of losing in trial, as well as performance and ongoing relationship of the parties after the trial.

These ADR processes are not only useful in legal disputes, but they are also useful in everyday life. In fact, we hear about them all the time on television, in books, in newspapers, and in the world around us. Negotiation for hostages, mediation in sports contracts, and arbitration in labor disputes have become commonplace.

The purpose of this book is to introduce you to negotiation, mediation, and arbitration in the legal system and in your everyday life.

CHAPTER 2

The Art of Negotiation

Negotiation is the act of settling a dispute between two individuals. Often negotiation involves the deliberation, discussion, or conference between two disputing individuals resulting in settlement of the conflict.

Some disputes involve opposing views on the same issue; the resolution of these disputes, can result in one

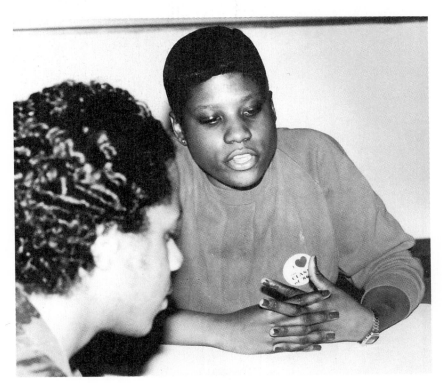

Often negotiation involves the deliberation, discussion, or conference between two disputing individuals resulting in settlement of the conflict.

person winning while the other loses, or a solution that meets both parties' needs or interests can be created. Sometimes disputes are just differences of opinion concerning how to solve a problem that comes up; these disputes require problem solving. Negotiation can be used to do both.

Negotiation is a process. This process can be described through a series of steps. At each step, the disputing individuals must make conscious choices that direct the next step. The ultimate goal is to resolve the dispute.

For this discussion, the terms **conflict** and **dispute** are used similarly. Those involved in the conflict are referred to as *individuals, persons,* or *parties.* In real life, individuals or persons can be **parties** in the dispute but so can companies or groups of individuals. Whether it is two or more individuals who oppose one another in a dispute, or whether it is groups, corporations, and nations that oppose one another, all are considered parties in the dispute.

The steps in negotiation can be defined as in Table 2–1.

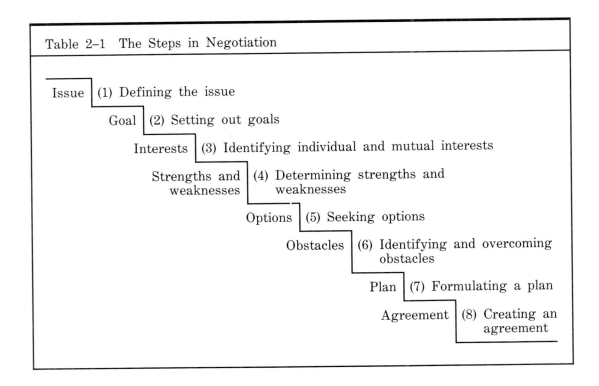

Table 2-1   The Steps in Negotiation

Issue — (1) Defining the issue

Goal — (2) Setting out goals

Interests — (3) Identifying individual and mutual interests

Strengths and weaknesses — (4) Determining strengths and weaknesses

Options — (5) Seeking options

Obstacles — (6) Identifying and overcoming obstacles

Plan — (7) Formulating a plan

Agreement — (8) Creating an agreement

Let's examine these steps in the context of a real case:

John wants to use the car on Saturday night, but his father says 'no'. What should he do?

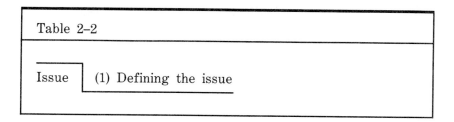

Table 2–2	
Issue	(1) Defining the issue

In negotiation, the parties may have a hard time defining the real issue. During this first step of defining the issue, each individual must stop and diagnose the situation. To do this, each must gather information, listen, organize the information, think about it, and try to use objective judgment in identifying the real issue.

Information gathering, listening, information organizing, thinking, and objective analysis are all part of identifying the issue. Information gathering means asking questions such as, "What really happened?", "Who is really involved?", "When did all this take place?", "Why is this a problem?", and "How did this arise now?" Listening is one of the most difficult skills in this process. It means not just sitting back and letting others have a turn to speak. It really means actively paying attention and trying to understand. Information organizing is done inside you. Based on what you learned and heard, you organize the information, think about it, and balancing all that you heard, identify the real issue.

You may think, "Issues are easy to identify." However, what *you* think is the issue may not be what another person thinks is the issue. In fact, that difference may be the basis for the dispute.

Many times individuals cannot focus on the issues. There are many reasons for this. The most common factors hindering individuals from focusing on or identifying issues are: lack of communication, failure to listen, lack of trust, different perspectives, threats, strong feelings, and lack of information.

Lack of Communication

Often individuals have used unclear communications or have not really communicated their real concerns at all. People sometimes believe that others should understand their position without really telling them what this position is. Other times individuals say things that are misinterpreted or unclear. Even when people communicate their concerns effectively, they may do so in ways that anger others or hinder real communication. All these difficulties get in the way of successful dispute resolution.

Failure to Listen

Even before a dispute, individuals may anticipate some problems and may have decided in advance what decision they prefer. This type of planning without, at a minimum, finding out the other person's views, tends to stop parties from listening while they propel their own point of view. The result is further conflict rather than its resolution. Though the individuals should have the opportunity to state their positions and interests, they should actively listen to each other as well. Good, sincere listening by both parties tends to decrease hostility and be more persuasive in getting the other person to consider each point of view.

Lack of Trust

Unhappy past dealings between people sometimes foster a lack of trust. Perhaps one person has said or done things in the past that have hurt another person's feelings or have left that person with ill will. The result is that future disputes are difficult to resolve. For this reason, disputes must be resolved so that parties walk away with a true sense of resolution. In this way, they may continue to interact successfully in the future.

Different Perspectives

Often different people have different points of view on the same issue. Some reasons for this difference are differences in ages, educational levels, or life experiences. As a result, well-intentioned, well-meaning individuals may have totally different perspectives on how a dispute should be resolved. One way to bridge this gap is to try to understand the other individual's perspective rather than just emphasizing one's own perspective.

Threats

Threats are often part of a dispute and may sound like, "You do things my way or else ...," or "Either you do it this way or...." Lawyers sometimes even say, "Do it this way or I'll sue you." The result is always the same. No dispute is resolved.

Strong Feelings

There are many issues about which individuals do not care, and there are many issues about which they care a great deal. Those issues about which individuals care a great deal certainly are important enough to explore and discuss at depth to reach a resolution. However, if people make every issue one about which they really care, the result is a day full of turmoil. Individuals themselves must determine what is or is not important to them before they try to resolve a dispute.

Lack of Information

Sometimes an individual hears about an event from another person and says, "How could he have done that?" or "How could he have said that?" Sometimes a person is told about a decision and says, "How could she have decided that?" or "Didn't she know about ...?" Making decisions or judgments without finding out all the information does not further resolution but rather furthers questions and mistrust.

The Case

John wants to use the car on Saturday night, but his father says no. What should he do?

John and his father present us with an example. John might say the problem is that his father is stubborn and never lets him use the car. John's father might say, "John is lazy. He is always asking for the car. John should spend more time studying and less time driving."

What is the real problem? John needs the car for his date with Linda at 8:00 on Saturday night. John's father needs the car to take John's mother to see a movie they both looked forward to seeing that night. The real problem is that both parties need the car at the same time on the same day. The individual who can identify this and *say* it will successfully focus the discussion and resolve it.

To successfully resolve this conflict, each party must continuously define the issue clearly without letting other opinions or feelings get in the way.

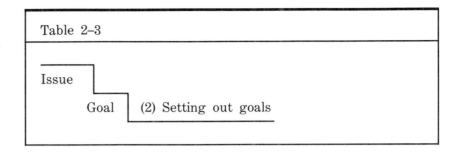

Table 2–3

Issue

Goal | (2) Setting out goals

In negotiation, each party must set out major **goals.**
This means that each party must understand the other
party's goal as well as his or her own. In a sense, each
person must perceive the **problem** as the other person
perceives it. To influence the outcome of the dispute, each
person must be able to see the problem not only from his
or her perspective, but also from the other person's point
of view. Then each must try to determine both his or her
own goals and those of the other individual.

In the case of John and his father, John's goal is to
use the car to take Linda out on a date. John's father
would like to use the car to take his wife to the movies.
Each of their goals might be able to be met rather than
having only one party get what he wants.

Each may have further minor goals. John may want
to win an argument for a change. John's father may
want to encourage John to spend more time studying in
school while using the car as a reward. Sometimes both
major goals and minor goals can be met, and if the right
solution is created, both parties may be able to meet all
their goals.

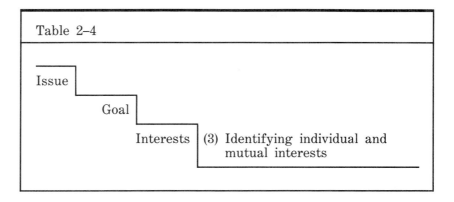

In negotiation, the individuals may have **interests** that they *say* and they may have interests that they *feel*. The dynamics of a conflict always involve these interests. Some interests may be more important to them than others. The individuals may have express interests about which they talk; they may have hidden interests about which they do not talk. They may have interests that are obviously related to the problem; they may also have interests that are only partially related to the problem. Identifying individual interests requires analyzing all these and sometimes talking about them.

In the case of John and his father, John may *say* his interest is to go on a date. He may *feel* he should get the car more often. John's father may *say* he must have the car to go to the movies. He may *feel* that a father's use of the car is more important than that of a child.

John's interest in going on a date with Linda, the prom queen, may be important to him. Perhaps he believes it is more important than the use of the car by his mother and father. John's father may think his interest in taking his wife out on Saturday is more important than a teenager's date.

John may say he wants the car for his date, but he may think the more often he gets the car on Saturday, the more likely he will get to use the car every Saturday.

John's father may say he must have the car on Saturday night, but he may think that giving the car to John all the time is not a good idea because John should be spending his time doing more constructive tasks, such as homework.

John's stated interest in using the car for a date is related to the problem; but John's statement that his father is stubborn and never gives him the car is only partially related to the problem. His father's interest in using the car to take his wife to the movies is related to the problem; but his statement that John should do less driving and more studying is only partially related to the problem.

Many express and hidden interests of the parties are part of a conflict's dynamic nature. Recognizing hidden and overt interests will help to solve the conflict.

Parties also have a mutual interest in getting along, having a peaceful, harmonious household and being able to live and work together in the family. John's case is no different from all disputes in that there are always shared mutual interests of the parties. Identifying not only individual interests, but also mutual interests brings everyone closer to resolving the dispute. At a minimum, in all disputes all the parties need and want mutual respect and understanding.

When trying to resolve a dispute it is critical for the parties to talk about what would happen if the dispute were not resolved. Clearly there are detrimental effects if a dispute is not resolved. It is in both parties' interest that the underlying conflict not continue. This is a critical, mutual interest.

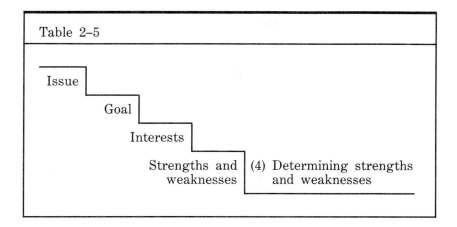

Table 2–5

Issue

    Goal

        Interests

            Strengths and | (4) Determining strengths
              weaknesses | and weaknesses

In negotiation, each party's case has certain strengths and weaknesses. These strengths and weaknesses can affect the outcome of the dispute. To reach a successful resolution to the dispute, each individual must anticipate and recognize the strengths and weaknesses of the other individual and those strengths and weaknesses he or she has.

In the problem of John and his father, John's weaknesses are that he does not own the car and that he is a child in the father-child relationship. John's strength is that he may be willing to go out of his way or do extra work to achieve his goal; he can afford to be flexible. His father's strengths are that he owns the car and that, in the family structure, he is the head of the household. His weakness may be his desire to maintain control over the family.

To solve this, John might say, "Dad, I think you may see giving me the car as a sign of fatherly weakness, but really I would very much appreciate it, and I'm willing to do extra work and help." To solve this, John's father might say, "You probably think I want to control you, but really I am just concerned that you spend your time wisely and not make the silly mistakes that I did. Perhaps we can work out some arrangement given that your time is more flexible." Either party has control over attempting to reach an agreement.

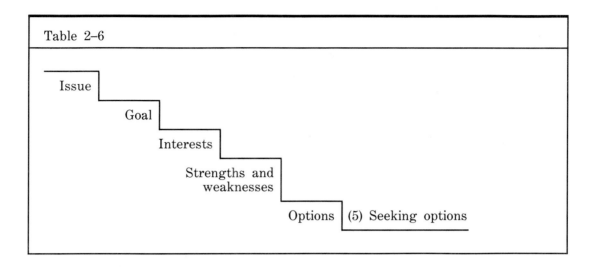

Table 2–6

Issue

Goal

Interests

Strengths and
weaknesses

Options | (5) Seeking options

In negotiation, an individual must consider all possible **options** that are available to both parties. All these options should be considered, including those beneficial to *both* sides. With each option, a person should ask, "Does this option meet the needs and interests of both parties?" Both persons must be willing to consider many solutions to the dispute.

One major goal in seeking options is to try to find an option or solution where both persons gain something as a result. Even if each person must compromise a little, if both parties feel they have won something, the solution can be considered most effective.

In the case of John and his father, John may be willing to drive his parents to the movie and pick them up. John may take the car on the promise that his parents could have the car on the following Saturday. John may offer to fill the tank with gas to get the use of the car. John's father may offer to go to the movies on Friday night so John could use the car on Saturday. The car may need some repair or oil change that John could do in exchange for use of the car. Or perhaps both couples could go to the same movie.

The results of creative options are that everyone wins something, no one walks away still angry, and a process is set up for resolving future conflicts.

Research also indicates that settling a dispute with an agreement from which each individual wins something encourages everyone to perform on the agreement. Alternatively when someone wins and someone loses, the losing party is less likely to perform on the agreement. Thus, to encourage settlement and performance generating options which benefit both parties is preferable.

Table 2-7

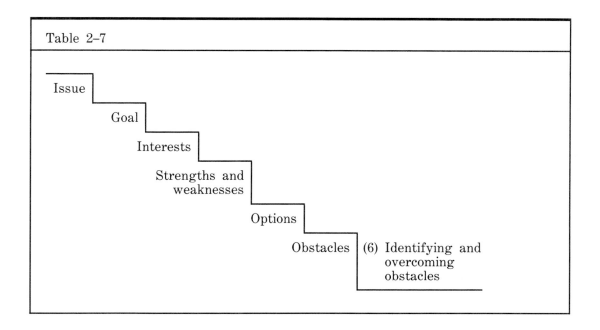

In negotiation, individuals must try to anticipate **obstacles** or problems that may come up in the course of the negotiation. Plans can be made to overcome those obstacles or decrease their effect on the successful outcome of the negotiation.

Some common obstacles to negotiation are: (1) hostility of the parties; (2) lack of agreement on any point; (3) personal bias; (4) threats; (5) power positioning; (6) accusations; (7) the "it's your problem" syndrome; and (8) refusal to consider views other than your own.

Skills can be learned to handle these obstacles:

(1) Hostility of the Parties

One way to decrease hostility is by simply addressing it. It helps to say, "I think there is much hostility between us, and perhaps we could come to a faster solution if we tried to deal with the underlying problem creating these negative feelings."

(2) Lack of Agreement

Often when an individual disagrees strongly with someone, then the individual tends to dislike anything about
the other person, including that person's tie, shoes, family, and so forth. At that point, resolution is impossible. It
may help to say, "There must be something on which we
agree. For example, what do you think about this great
weather we're having?" Finding points of agreement helps
to resolve conflicts.

(3) Personal Bias

If an individual has had poor experiences with certain
people or has heard about poor experiences from others,
that individual tends to expect similar poor experiences in
future dealings with those people. This kind of thinking
sets up biases that may affect how individuals settle or
deal with disputes. By recognizing personal biases and
focusing on the problem or issue instead, bias is
decreased.

(4) Threats

Sometimes people say things that hurt others. Threats of
any kind tend to do this. If a person can identify the
threat and indicate the hurt rather than retaliate with
another threat, the person has successfully handled it.
Saying, for example, "That hurts my feelings, and it
doesn't help our real problem, which is ..." may help.

(5) Power Positioning

"I'm the landlord, so we'll do things my way," or "I'm
the mother, so what I say will be the answer." How
often have we heard people state their position as power
in a dispute? To deal with this, one cannot negate this
power but recognize it, while at the same time, indicate
that some weaknesses in that position or the uncertainties
of a problem could be best handled in another way. This

might include joining and acting with others who have the same problem, pointing out the weaknesses of the individual in power, or suggesting that others in the family or community may not like what is happening. One might say, "I understand you are the landlord and this is your building, but a number of tenants are concerned about this. Rather than make this problem any worse or get more community members involved, perhaps it is in everyone's interest if we try to resolve it amicably to everyone's satisfaction."

(6) Accusations

Whether the accusations are true or not, trying to understand the other party, their motivations, and their concerns helps to reach agreements. Asking questions instead of responding to accusations helps to do this. For example, instead of saying "I am not a liar, you thief", ask "Why did you call me a liar?" Then listen to the response and discuss the problem rationally.

(7) The "It's Your Problem" Syndrome

"This is your problem, not mine" is often stated by one party in a dispute. These individuals must be convinced that what appears to be problems of others could also happen to them. Further, though they think they are right, they may be proven wrong. That is why everyone involved with an issue must get involved in solving it.

(8) Other Perspectives

Though individuals may think they are right, it pays to hear other people's points of view. They may actually agree or come up with a better solution.

Chapter 3 deals with all these obstacles and offers more methods of solving them.

In John's case, John may attack his father personally, call him names, or wield accusations at him; his father may do the same to John. Both may become very hostile and may even stop talking to one another. If John asks his father how he might take his date out without the car, his father might say, "John, that's your problem." All these events are obstacles to successful negotiation and, therefore, must be either decreased or eliminated for the negotiation to be successful.

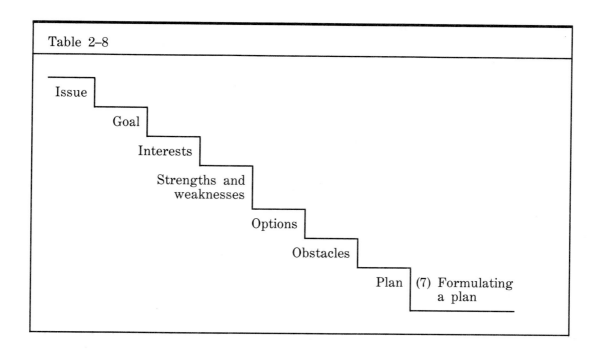

Table 2–8

Issue

Goal

Interests

Strengths and
weaknesses

Options

Obstacles

Plan   (7) Formulating
a plan

In negotiation, formulating a **plan** to resolve disputes depends to a great extent on two factors: your style and your method. Different styles will be discussed in this chapter. Different methods are discussed in Chapter 3.

Your Style or Approach

Negotiation consists of generally two basic styles or approaches: competitive and cooperative. Individuals can use either style or both, but they should be aware of each of them and use them depending on the issue involved.

The first style is that of being competitive. In using this style, individuals try to put themselves at an advantage while putting the other party at a disadvantage. As soon as one side appears weak or disorganized, the competitive party takes advantage. In this situation, the competitive party tries to win while making the other party lose. The competitive party often wants to get the most possible even if it is to the disadvantage of the opponent. In the short run, the competitive party may appear to "win," but in the long run, this style is less effective than the second style: being cooperative.

A second style approach in negotiation is that of being cooperative. Cooperative negotiators think of alternatives that will allow each party to win something. They try to see the opposing party's point of view and create a solution that meets the other party's needs while meeting their own needs. Every effort is made to maximize winning for both parties. Though the ultimate agreement may involve some compromise on both sides, each party will believe that he or she has won something. Success using this style lies in one person finding out what the other person really wants and showing that person a way to get it while both get what they want.

Here are some sample discussions:
The competitive style . . .

Mark: "You are totally wrong on this issue. You can't even keep your appointments, so how can we expect you to solve this problem?"

Richard: "I called you in advance to tell you there would be a time conflict. You agreed to postpone the meeting. Now how can you use that as a way to make me agree to your point?"

The cooperative style . . .

Mark: "Though I do not agree with your view of the issue, I can understand why you might feel that way. However, we have been able to handle other difficulties that have occurred, such as the time you thought there might be a time problem for our meeting, so we agreed to postpone it. I think we can come to some fair solution on this issue."

Richard: "You are right. We have been able to handle other difficulties. Let's look at both our interests and see if we can come up with a solution that we can both live with."

In John's case, John may want to use a cooperative rather than a competitive style with his father. His father, however, may see this dispute as a competition for the use of the car and may very well want to win. John may have to point out to his father, "I know we both want to win, Dad, but we could both really win if we could find a solution that would meet both our needs." A successful solution will have to benefit both of them.

Your Method

A good negotiator can use a number of methods to achieve success in negotiation. These methods include: The Nice Guy method, the Teach Me method, the Investment Partner method, the Creative Problem Solver method, the Compete method, and the Combat method. They are described in Chapter 3.

Table 2–9

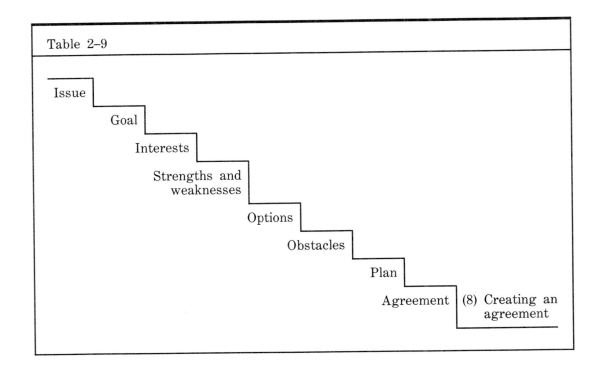

In negotiation, a final solution that meets both parties' needs while resolving the dispute must be created. The solution is incorporated into an **agreement.** Sometimes the parties also set out some penalties or alternatives in the context of the settlement if the agreement is not kept by one of the parties in the future.

In the case of John and his father, John may promise to fill the gas tank with gas and give his father the car the following Saturday. His father may agree to this on the basis that if John does not keep his promises, he will not be able to use the car for a month. However, if John does keep his promise, he will be able to use the car other Saturday nights.

Conclusion

All negotiations require defining the issue, setting out goals, identifying individual interests, determining strengths and weaknesses, seeking options, identifying and overcoming obstacles, formulating a plan, and creating an agreement.

Some obstacles to defining the issue include lack of communication, failure to listen, lack of trust, different perspectives, threats, strong feelings, and lack of information.

When setting out goals, individuals must identify not only their own goal, but also that of the other party in the dispute.

People in conflict have express and hidden interests. A good resolution of a conflict takes into consideration the express and hidden interests of both parties.

Each party's case has certain strengths and weaknesses that should be considered and discussed in the negotiation process.

Many options should be considered by the parties when seeking a resolution to the dispute. The best options will allow each party to win something.

Obstacles to resolving conflicts include hostility, lack of agreement, personal bias, threats, power positioning, accusations, the "it's your problem" syndrome, and refusal to consider other perspectives. These obstacles must be addressed before disputes can be resolved.

Negotiation consists of generally two basic styles: competitive and cooperative.

A good final agreement meets the needs of both parties.

Exercises

The following conflicts range from the simple to the complex: from interpersonal and community disputes to corporate and global conflicts. The problems are intended to show that similar steps and processes involving apparently simpler disputes, such as that between a father and a son, are also applicable to corporate, community, and global disputes.

In each conflict below, identify all the steps in a negotiation: (1) the real problem, (2) the goals of the parties, (3) the individual interests, (4) each party's strengths and weaknesses, (5) some possible outcomes, (6) some obstacles and how they can be overcome, (7) some plans to deal with the dispute, and (8) some possible agreements.

Remember: There is no one right answer to disputes. Disputes can often be solved in many ways.

Conflict 1

You want to borrow $20 from your mother, but y͏̶
mother says no. How can this be resolved?

Conflict 2

You apply for a job but cannot even get an interview.
How can this be resolved?

Conflict 3

Your neighbor plays loud music every night, and you cannot stop him. How can this be resolved?

Conflict 4

John just intentionally pushed you in the hall. How can
this be resolved?

Conflict 5

Steve failed the English examination and will therefore be ineligible to play on the football team. The semester ends in two weeks. How can this be resolved?

Conflict 6

You owe the gas company money, and it is going to disconnect your heat. You do not have the money. How can this be resolved?

Conflict 7

The Village Board wants to increase property taxes. The new tax money would be used to fix decaying schools and park facilities. Opponents of the proposition do not have children in schools, do not use the parks, and would not like to spend money for taxes. How can this be resolved?

Conflict 8

Home Steel Corporation has suffered profit losses within the last year due to increased cost of raw materials. As a result, management has proposed that future pay raises will be suspended or 10 percent of the employees will be laid off. Union leaders are angry. They contend the cost-of-living increase requires pay raises, and they are opposed to any workers losing their jobs. How can this be resolved?

Conflict 9

A Cuban trolling and drilling rig was stationed in international waters just outside the designated twelve-mile limit of the U.S. territorial waters. In the course of its drilling, the Cuban vessel struck oil and is now claiming oil rights on behalf of Cuba. The United States contends that the boat was within the twelve-mile limit, given measurement changes and wind currents. Therefore, the United States claims oil rights. Cuba is currently going through an economic depression, and the oil rights could make a substantial difference on its economy. How can this be resolved?

*Prior to negotiating, think through the problem and the
steps leading to an outcome.*

Negotiation Plan

The Negotiation Plan was developed to use prior to an actual negotiation of a dispute. Its purpose is to provide a step-by-step plan to follow. In this way, you can think through the problem and the steps leading to its outcome prior to entering into negotiations.

Negotiation Plan

Name: _____

Problem: _____

Your side's name: _____

Other side's name: _____

1. What is the problem?

_____

_____

_____

_____

_____

_____

_____

2. What are the goals of each party?

Your Goals	Their Goals

3. How would you prioritize your goals?

    Absolutely crucial   _____

    _____

    _____

    Generally important   _____

    _____

    _____

    Would like to have   _____

    _____

    _____

4. What interests does each side have?

Your Interests	Their Interests
Main interests:_____	Main interests:_____
_____	_____
_____	_____
_____	_____
_____	_____
Possible hidden interests:	Possible hidden interests:
_____	_____
_____	_____
_____	_____

5. What strengths does each side have?

      Your Strengths   Their Strengths

6. What weaknesses does each side have?

      Your Weaknesses   Their Weaknesses

7. What are the options? (List all options, including those that you may not use.)

    A. _____

    B. _____

    C. _____

    D. _____

8. What obstacles do you think may have to be overcome?

    A. _____

    B. _____

    C. _____

    D. _____

9. What plan will you use?

A. _____

B. _____

C. _____

D. _____

10. What research and preparation have you done?

_____

_____

_____

_____

Result: _____

_____

_____

_____

_____

_____

_____

_____

_____

_____

CHAPTER **3**

Methods

Negotiation is a process of settling disputes by satisfying one party's underlying concerns, interests, and needs *and* those of the other party.

There are many ways of doing this. These methods can be called the Nice Guy method, the Teach Me method, the Investment Partner method, the Creative Problem Solver method, the Compete method, and the Combat method. Often during the course of a conflict, more than one of these methods may be used by either party.

The Nice Guy Method

Mr. Nice Guy gives in because he wants to be liked. He first appears reasonable and soft-spoken, but he is too quick to give up his own goals and needs. He will be flexible and agreeable, but in the process, he is giving up everything including things the other party never wanted. Mr. Nice Guy may originally say he has some key points he wants. During the course of the negotiation, however, he cannot stand confrontations and discord, so he gives up everything for peace. In doing so, he hurts himself.

The Teach Me Method

Ms. Teach Me is not stupid; in fact, she is highly intelligent. She has learned that when she asks questions and admits she does not know information, the other party usually is willing to forget anger or hostility and talk to her. She is always asking questions such as, "I'm sorry, I don't understand. Could you explain this? What does this word mean? What do you mean by that? Huh? I am con-

A good negotiator can use a number of methods to achieve success in negotiation. These methods include: the Nice Guy method, the Teach Me method, the Investment Partner method, the Creative Problem Solver method, the Compete method, and the Combat method.

fused. Could you help me with this?" These questions immediately put the other party at ease and make the other party feel as though he or she should help Ms. Teach Me. In doing so, hostility is replaced by a helping attitude, and Ms. Teach Me can work more effectively with the other party. Through this method, Ms. Teach Me also learns a great deal about the needs and interests of the other party.

The Investment Partner Method

Mr. Investment Partner is prepared well in advance before a confrontation with the other party. He has determined what he would like to get out of this negotiation, and he has taken the time to determine what the other party would probably like to get out of this negotiation. He has figured out express interests and hidden interests. He believes both parties should invest in the successful outcome of this problem, because both parties have the opportunity to gain from this investment. When he meets with the other party, he begins by pointing out why settling this conflict is to the advantage of the other party and to himself. He points out that each party has a stake in the successful resolution of the conflict, and because the stake is so high, each party should work diligently to reach a successful resolution to the problem.

The Creative Problem Solver Method

Ms. Creative Problem Solver knows the other party's views. She also realizes that the views appear to be in total opposition to her perspective. This, however, does not bother her. She is determined to come to the negotiation table with a range of possible creative solutions that the other party most likely has not even considered. She is creative and ingenious. Some of her solutions are, admittedly, "far out," but many of them are intriguing and reasonable. The other party is caught off guard by these somewhat new possibilities and is willing to consider them as possible outcomes to the problem, provided he or she gets something, too. When both parties consider other options to problem solving, they are concentrating on the problem not the people, and they put their anger aside. During negotiation, Ms. Creative Problem Solver always reminds us, "The real problem is . . . and some possible ways to solve it are. . . ."

The Compete Method

Mr. Compete is a tough individual with whom to deal. He is always interested in showing the other party that he is better and he is right. The problem is not as important to him as is winning. He wants to walk away from the negotiation believing he has won something while the other party has really lost. A win-lose approach is the story of his life. He wants to win more points than the other guy. He keeps score. He would be happiest with an outcome where he could say he really won while the other party had to give in and lose. He needs to be able to say he did something right and got something good.

The Combat Method

Ms. Combat is agreeable to only one solution, her solution. She is determined to have her way at all costs. Even if the other party indicates a willingness to give in a little or be reasonable, Ms. Combat sees this as a sign of weakness and further insists on her point of view. She does not budge from her stance. If the other party gives up one point totally, Ms. Combat does not think she is required to give up something, also. Rather, she generally ignores this concession and further insists on her view. She later laughs and brags about how she got the other party to concede a point while she maintained her position. To her, winning her way is everything. Unfortunately, the losing party is completely devastated, will remain angry for a long time, and may try to get even. The losing party may refuse to carry out the agreement.

During Negotiation: Who Should You Be?

During negotiation, most people are not any one of these, but are a combination. Good negotiators know these different methods and will use them when they feel they would be most effective in resolving a particular conflict.

For example, most people may begin by being Mr. Nice Guy or Ms. Teach Me. They may be ready with creative solutions, like Ms. Creative Problem Solver, and they may often point out how each party has a stake in the outcome of the dispute, like Mr. Investment Partner. Mr. Compete and Ms. Combat may enjoy winning, but their approaches do not always solve problems; in fact, the probability of the parties coming to an agreement at all is small. They believe, however, that though they have a small chance of winning, if they do win, they will win everything they want while the other party will totally lose.

Conclusion

In the negotiation process, a combination of methods are usually used in dealing with different issues.

Exercises

Students should choose one method and try to negotiate with one another on the following problems. In each case, after the negotiations, the class should discuss how effective each method is in solving the conflict.

Conflict 1

You want to borrow $20 from your father for a date, but your father says no. In fact, he has a general rule that you should work to pay for your own dates.

Conflict 2

You want to use the car for the day to go somewhere with your friends. However, your grandmother must do some shopping and pick up some medicine she needs. You know shopping with grandmother takes so long that you would not have time to do anything with your friends.

Conflict 3

Your mother owes money to the county for a water bill. The county will shut off your water if this bill is not paid. It is summer time and water is scarce. Your mother just lost her job. A meeting with the county agent is scheduled.

Conflict 4

Your little brother, eight years old, is in third grade and is flunking reading. Because of this, his teacher is considering failing him. Your mother has been crying for days about this. Your brother just took the final exam and failed. He asked for your help at a conference with the teacher scheduled for tomorrow.

Conflict 5

The president of K Corporation has refused to give raises this year to her employees. She says that the company has not made a profit because of stiff competition and, therefore, she cannot give raises. The union leader representing all the employees believes the employees will be extremely angry if they do not get a raise, considering the cost of living has gone up 7 percent. Further, he will lose his position as union leader if he cannot go back to the employees and tell them what he got for them as a result of negotiating with the president of the corporation.

Conflict 6

Representatives from Sweden are meeting with representatives from Finland. Each country has claimed fishing rights in the Gulf of Bothnia. The people from each of these countries who have been fishing in the gulf have been arrested by the other country for trespassing. Fish is a major source of food to both countries not only for their people, but also for export to other countries. Represent both countries in this negotiation.

CHAPTER 4

Obstacles to Negotiation

When two parties are embroiled in a dispute, a number of obstacles can get in the way of resolving the problem. If the parties can recognize these obstacles, they will be able to deal with them more effectively and can even overcome them.

Hostility

Most parties in a conflict are angry. This hostility often appears to escalate or increase rather than disappear or decrease during the course of a dispute. When hostility increases, it affects behavior; some people yell, cry, or even use violence or force. Even after a negotiation when one person loses and one person wins, the loser may still be unhappy or hostile. When the parties remain hostile, no dispute is really resolved. Hostility is an obstacle to dispute resolution.

One way to deal with hostility is to say, "I feel both of us are angry, and I don't think we can resolve the issue until we deal with this." Addressing your concerns or those of the other party is critical to decreasing hostility.

Lack of Agreement

When parties are in conflict, they do not appear to agree on anything. They are so angry that often they are not even listening to one another. Even if one party might say something with which the other party might agree, he or she would probably say he or she does not agree on that point or any point. Lack of agreement is an obstacle to negotiation.

One way to handle this is to point out on what you both do agree. For example, "It sounds as though we're in total disagreement on ... but we were able to agree to discuss this, and we were able to find some time together, so let us see where we are in agreement on this."

Personal Bias

During the dispute, one party may call the other party names or may even refer to the other party as "you people." This often happens even during conflicts between neighbors or relatives. Workers, for example, refer to management leaders by saying, "You people don't understand us." This we-you mentality is a real obstacle in conflict resolution.

The focus of any discussion should be the issues, not the people. To overcome this obstacle, point out the real issues of the case and ask that people issues not be part of the discussion.

Threats

People in conflict often use threats against one another. Threats rarely solve conflicts and generally escalate bad feelings. People often say, "If you don't do it my way, I will sue you." Realistically, they may hesitate to pay a lawyer or take the time to go to court, but threats seem like a good way to get back at the other party.

Threats never solve a dispute. In dealing with this obstacle, you might say, "Threats will not solve our real problem. Let's see if we can deal with the real issues."

Focus on Positions

Many times the parties are in certain positions where they have unequal bargaining power. For example, the landlord may appear to have more power than the tenant who has not paid the rent. The president of a company may appear to have more power than the employee working on the assembly line. The teacher may appear to have more power than the student. The parent may appear to have more power than the child. The store manager may appear to have more power than the customer. Yet, in each of these cases, the power of the apparently weaker party may be strengthened, while the position of the stronger party may be weakened.

The weaker party must examine his or her possible strengths. Perhaps he or she is a member of a group, and the group can act together powerfully. Perhaps the weaker party has special skills to offer in exchange during the negotiation. Perhaps the weaker party has time to offer. Alternatively, the stronger party may not really be able to afford to go to court. Or perhaps he or she does not have time to deal with a problem. Perhaps the stronger party could be reached through public opinion or another person who is stronger yet. Both parties have both strengths and weaknesses despite their apparent positions.

Accusations

Accusations are often hurled by both parties against one another during the course of a conflict. Often, these accusations are false or possibly have just a hint of truth. If all the facts were known, however, many accusations usually prove unfounded or are rarely the cause of the dispute. The result is increased hostility and anger, putting one party on the defensive and creating an environment wherein conflict resolution is unlikely.

Accusations never solve the problem. To overcome this obstacle, you might want to point out that fact. You may say, "Look, you can threaten me; I can threaten you. You can call me names; I can call you names. You can say I did this; I can say you did that. However, nothing will be resolved. Let's try to deal with the real *issues* and what to do *now*."

The "It's Your Problem" Syndrome

When one party may lose something if the negotiations fail, the other party may say, "Well, too bad. It's your problem. I don't have to deal with it because I have nothing to lose." This is an obstacle in that one party feels powerless because he or she may lose something and, furthermore, the other party knows it. However in reality, both parties may be afraid to lose something.

One party may not realize what the other party's weaknesses might be. To hide these, the other party may shift the burden of the entire problem onto the first party. This creates not only a win-lose situation, but it also creates an environment where one party does not even want to sit down to negotiate at all.

Making the problem everyone's problem is part of successful negotiation. To do this, point out what is at stake and why everyone should be concerned.

Refusal to Consider Other Views

Everyone likes to believe he or she is "right" while the other party is "wrong." The "right" people think they must win because they are right. However, sometimes the people who think they are "right" do not have all the facts, are misinformed, or do not realize that another view of the problem may have equal validity.

Good listening to the other party's views is just as important as stating one's own views. Both parties may have some good points. These good points should be commended and used in the agreement.

What Happens if No Agreement is Reached?

If all parties are stuck and agreement seems unlikely, each party should consider what will happen next if no agreement is reached. Greater cost? More time? More anger and hostility? Enlarging the dispute? Are the parties willing to face what will happen next? When the parties face the question, "What will happen if no agreement is reached?" they may come to the conclusion that what will happen next is worse than trying to work out an agreement through negotiation. Each party must remind the other throughout the negotiation of the costs and benefits of settling the dispute quickly or risk escalating the dispute if no agreement is reached.

Conclusion

Obstacles to negotiation must be resolved before disputes can be successfully settled. Some obstacles include hostility, lack of agreement, personal bias, threats, focusing on positions, accusations, the "it's your problem" syndrome, and refusal to consider other views. Throughout the negotiation each party must consider what will happen if no agreement is reached. The costs may outweigh the benefits.

Exercises

Try to determine the obstacles to negotiation in the following conflicts.

Conflict 1

John: You just want me to study more. That's why you won't let me have the car.

Father: You are lazy and no good. Of course you cannot use the car.

Conflict 2

Mary: You were in charge of creating the new project, and because the project has problems now, you must have created them.

Janet: New projects are going to meet with problems. We knew there would be problems when we began the project. If things don't go smoothly, it's easy to blame the people instead of realizing it's part of developing a new project. Now that there are problems, you want to blame them on me. Address the problem instead.

Conflict 3

Company president: Our corporation cannot work with people like you. You are always trying to ruin the company and cost us money. We will go out of business because of people like you.

Union leader: You don't understand what it's like to work day in and day out on the assembly line. You make $1 million a year and sit behind a desk all day long.

Conflict 4

Landlord: Finding a new apartment is your problem. If you cannot pay your rent, you cannot live here.

Tenant: You think you're always right. You know there are many problems with this building. I could report you to City Hall.

Conflict 5

Student A: I know she meant to push me in the hall. I'm right because intentional pushing is not allowed.

Student B: Someone pushed me from behind. I certainly didn't want to hurt her. As soon as I ran into her, however, she would not listen and kept yelling at me. Why bother explaining anything to her?

CHAPTER 5

Overcoming Obstacles

To overcome obstacles to negotiation, a good negotiator thinks of ways to address these problems with a number of techniques. These techniques, however, must be in the mind of the negotiator throughout the negotiation so they can be used at any given moment an obstacle arises.

Focus on Interests

When parties are hostile and are even attacking each other personally, one technique for changing the direction of the conversation is to focus on the real issues and each party's interests. One might say, "I know you are angry. I am angry, too. But the real issue is whether you will evict me from my apartment. Your interest is in getting the rent. My interest is in staying in the apartment with my family. Let's focus on those issues."

This is not as easy as it seems. When both parties are angry, it is hard for either of them to stop screaming and focus on issues and interests. Yet, this is a way to overcome obstacles to successful negotiation.

Points of Agreement

Though it may appear that both parties do not agree on any single point, they must both agree on something, even if it is the weather or the date/time of the negotiation. They may agree that both would be worse off if the conflict is not settled, so they might as well try to settle it. Rather than continuing to argue point by point, they should stop and examine issues on which both parties agree. These may be little points rather than the key issue in dispute. Then after agreeing, both parties are in a better position to begin to resolve the major issue.

What if We Don't Agree?

Before entering into negotiations, an individual should determine what would happen if no agreement is reached. Also, an individual should determine what might happen if an agreement can be reached. Comparing these outcomes will help individuals in creating their goals. It will also help them during the negotiations in redirecting the other party by pointing out what would happen if an agreement is or is not reached.

Ask Questions

To argue when someone is sincerely asking for help is hard. Sometimes the best way for parties to overcome obstacles in negotiation is for one party to stop arguing and start sincerely asking questions. He or she might begin by saying, "Could I ask a few questions?" or "I don't understand something. Could you explain?" This shifts the discussion from argument to issues and information gathering.

Listening is a skill essential to effective communication. Let the other party know that you are interested in what he or she is saying. Sit close to the table instead of leaning away. Look eye to eye, rest your hands on the table and plant your legs firmly on the floor.

Listen

Listening is a skill that is essential to effective communication. Listening is also a useful technique to overcoming obstacles to negotiation. When parties are fighting, they are usually so busy talking or yelling that they do not stop to listen to one another. Sometimes one party may even be presenting a good solution or a valid point for consideration. By listening, a good negotiator can pick up on this point and use it during the course of the negotiation. Sometimes by listening, a party can find out information he or she did not know before that will further help in negotiation. Indicate you are listening, and the other party will listen to you.

Trust

Trust is a difficult technique to use during negotiation but is highly successful. Rather than quarreling, good negotiators may say that they trust the other party and that they hope the other party will try to trust them, too. They may point out that both parties want a reasonable solution and both parties will benefit if the negotiation is successful. For that reason, they will have to begin to trust one another. Good negotiators may also point out that the alternatives, if the problem is not resolved, are worse than negotiation, so the parties had better begin to trust one another. Trust is an essential factor in negotiation, particularly when the parties will have to continue to work or live together.

Identify Alternatives

Many times each party in the dispute believes his or her way of solving the dispute is the only "right" way. One person does not always take the time to see the other person's point of view. In fact, the other person may have some valid points. There may also be some additional facts that are yet unknown. Therefore, by having a limited view, that person does not always take the time to consider a whole range of possible alternatives that are available. For example, the employee may say the only way to resolve the dispute between the union and the company management is to give the employees a raise. The company president may insist that the only fair way of resolving the dispute is to hold the line on the wage freeze so the company will not suffer economic hardship. Neither may have considered other possible alternatives such as offering employees stock in the company, better health benefits, a life insurance plan, bonus trips for extra work, or other fringe benefits rather than salary raises. The employees may accept these alternatives rather than a wage increase, and some of these may cost the company management very little. Therefore, whenever parties are in conflict and both consider their way the only "right" way to solve it, parties may consider examining a whole range of alternatives to overcome this obstacle. Alternatives that are mutually beneficial are more likely to resolve the dispute.

Fairness

The parties' consideration of fairness might have to change for a solution to result. What is fair in the eyes of one party may not be considered fair to another party. For example, in a dispute between a landlord and a tenant, the tenant refused to pay the rent because the landlord was two months late in repairing things in the apartment. The landlord believed the tenant was not fair in withholding the rent. The tenant felt the landlord was not fair in delaying the repairs. The landlord admitted that he was behind in repairs, but he was fixing things as quickly as he could. He needed tenant rent money to pay the mortgage on his building. The tenant believed the landlord should fix things quicker and that by withholding the rent, the landlord might be more motivated to fix things. In this case, each party believed his solution was the fairer one.

If, however, the parties moved away from concentrating on money and concentrated on the problem itself, another "fair" solution might result. For example, if the tenant could offer to help the landlord repair other much needed building problems in exchange for rent, both parties will win and a fairer result will be achieved. Thus, how one measures fairness should be examined closely to overcome obstacles in negotiation.

Attack the Problem, Not the Person

Oftentimes during the course of a negotiation, parties wind up attacking each other personally rather than focusing their attention on the issue. To overcome this obstacle, the parties must shift from attacking each other to attacking the issues. This process may begin when one party redefines issues and reminds the other that therein lies the successful resolution of the problem. This statement may have to be done frequently, particularly if the conflict has escalated to the point where the parties are not speaking to one another. By shifting from attacking the person to attacking the problem, successful resolution is much more likely.

Find a Solution That Benefits Both Parties

Creative solutions may benefit both parties. For example, both parties can "brainstorm" some other ways to solve the problem. To do this, they list all the possibilities and then identify those that will benefit both parties. They may come with a list of creative options. They may package the options in such a way that the solution appears more acceptable. Solutions that are mutually beneficial to both parties are more likely to resolve the dispute.

Conclusion

To overcome obstacles in negotiation, a negotiator addresses problems using a number of techniques. These techniques include focusing on interests, finding points of agreement, determining why it is in everyone's best interest to settle the dispute, asking questions, listening, indicating trust, identifying alternatives, showing fairness, attacking the problem, and finding a solution that benefits both parties.

Exercises

Examine the conflicts in Chapter 3 and try to use these methods of overcoming obstacles.

Outside-of-Class Fun

Look through the daily newspapers for articles about conflicts. Find articles where parties, companies, or countries are negotiating; where mediators are called in to resolve a dispute; where two parties cannot seem to agree; or where a dispute went to arbitration.

Using Historical Conflicts as Examples

Ask your teacher about historical conflicts and discuss how they could have been resolved.

CHAPTER **6**

Creative
Negotiations

Creative Outcomes

Many times it takes a creative problem solver to resolve conflicts in a way that meets both parties' interests and needs. This chapter examines some negotiations found in literature. When reading about them, try to identify the issue, the goals, the interests, the strengths and weaknesses, the options, the obstacles, the plan, and the agreement.

* * *

In the following case, one party identifies his goal but it may not be his *real* goal.

The Tale of Brer Rabbit

Adapted from *Nights with Uncle Remus* by Joel Chandler Harris

Brer Rabbit had got himself caught by Brer Fox and was well on his way to becoming evening dinner. Brer Rabbit was in a great deal of deep trouble. And all because he tried to win a fight with a tar baby.

There did not seem much he could do about this one, but he did not seem concerned at all at being the Fox's dinner. He just said:

> *"Brer Fox, I don't mind if you eat me. But oh, whatever you do, don't throw me in that briar patch."*

Now Brer Fox was surely looking forward to eating his old enemy, but he was curiouser and curiouser about Brer Rabbit's sweating and crying about being thrown into the briar patch.

The more he questioned it, the more Brer Rabbit wailed about how much he hated and feared that briar patch.

Pretty soon it did seem that Brer Rabbit would rather be eaten than be set among those briars. So Brer Fox threw Brer Rabbit right into the briar patch.

Brer Fox hung around to see what was going to happen. By-and-by he heard somebody call him and way up the hill he saw Brer Rabbit.

"Bred and born in the briar patch, Brer Fox!"

Then Brer Fox knew that he had been fooled mighty badly.

What people say may not be what they want. Find out what they really want. Ask for clarification.

---

* * *

In the story of *Dividing A Baby,* the parties could not resolve a dispute so they went to an arbitrator, King Solomon.

Dividing A Baby

From *The Bible Story* by Arthur Maxwell

One of the first problems the new King Solomon met was a very difficult one. Two women came to him, both claiming the same baby. They wanted him to decide whose it was.

Sitting on his throne, Solomon listened carefully to their story. The two women lived together in the same house. Their babies had been born about the same time, one three days before the other. Then one of the babies had died.

Said the first woman, "O my lord, this woman's child died in the night. And she arose at midnight and took my son from beside me, while thine handmaid slept, and laid her dead child next to me. When I awoke in the morning to feed my baby, I found a dead child in my arms which was not mine but the other woman's child."

"No!" cried the other woman frantically, "The living is my son and the dead is thy son!"

Poor Solomon! He truly needed wisdom in this case.

"Bring me a sword," he said calmly, and a servant brought him one, while silence fell over the room. "Now the baby!" said the King.

There was a gasp.

"Divide the living child in two," said Solomon, "and give half to the one and half to the other."

Everyone was shocked.

"No! Please don't!" screamed the real mother. "O my lord, give her the living child, and in no way slay it."

"No," said the other woman, "let it be neither mine nor thine, but divide it."

"Aha!" mused Solomon. "Now I know to whom the child belongs." Then pointing to the woman who had asked that the baby's life be spared, he said, "Give her the living child and in no way slay it. She is the mother thereof."

> *Look for ways to solve problems creatively.*

* * *

Mark Twain wrote about Tom Sawyer's ability to negotiate with his friends in order to get a job done.

Fence Whitewashing

From *The Adventures of Tom Sawyer*
by Mark Twain

(Like many of us who have been told to do something we do not want to do, Tom Sawyer was told by his aunt that he could not play because he had to whitewash the fence.)

(Tom) began to think of the fun he had planned for this day, and his sorrows multiplied. Soon the free boys would come tripping along on all sorts of delicious expeditions, and they would make a world of fun of him for having to work—the very thought of it burnt like fire....

He took up his brush and went tranquilly to work. Ben Rogers was in sight presently—the very boy, of all boys, whose ridicule he had been dreading. Ben's gait was the hop-skip-and-jump-proof enough that his heart was light and his anticipations high. He was eating an apple, and giving a long, melodious whoop, at intervals, followed by a deep-toned ding-dong-dong, for he was personating a steamboat, the Big Missouri....

Tom went on whitewashing—paid no attention to the steamboat. Ben stared a moment and then said:

"Hi-hi! You're up a stump, ain't you?"

No answer. Tom surveyed his last touch with an eye of an artist; then he gave his brush another gentle sweep and surveyed the result as before. Ben ranged up alongside of him. Tom's mouth watered for the apple but he stuck to his work. Ben said:

"Hello, old chap, you got work, hey?"

Tom wheeled suddenly and said:

"Why, it's you, Ben! I warn't noticing."

"Say—I'm going in a-swimming, I am. Don't you wish you could? But of course you'd druther work, wouldn't you? Course you would!"

Tom contemplated the boy a bit, and said:

"What do you call work?"

"Why, ain't that work?"

Tom resumed his whitewashing, and answered carelessly:

"Well, maybe it is, and maybe it ain't. All I know is, it suits Tom Sawyer."

"Oh, come now, you don't mean to let on that you like it?"

The brush continued to move.

"Like it? Well, I don't see why I oughtn't to like it. Does a boy get a chance to whitewash a fence every day?"

That put the thing in a new light. Ben stopped nibbling his apple. Tom swept his brush daintily back and forth—stepped back to note the effect—added a touch here and there—criticized the effect again—Ben watching every move and getting more and more interested, more and more absorbed. Presently he said:

"Say, Tom, let me whitewash a little."

Tom considered, was about to consent; but he altered his mind:

"No—no—I reckon it wouldn't hardly do, Ben. You see, Aunt Polly's awful particular about this fence right here on the street, you know—but if it was a back fence I wouldn't mind and she wouldn't. Yes, she's awful particular about this fence; it's got to be done very carefully; I reckon there ain't one boy in a thousand, maybe two thousand, that can do it the way it's got to be done."

"No—is that so? Oh, come, now—lemme just try. Only just a little—I'd let you, if you was me, Tom."

"Ben, I'd like to, honest injun; but Aunt Polly—well, Jim wanted to do it, but she wouldn't let him; Sid wanted to do it, and she wouldn't let Sid. Now don't you see how I'm fixed? If you was to tackle this fence and anything was to happen to it—"

"Oh, shucks, I'll be just as careful. Now lemme try. Say—I'll give you the core of my apple."

"Well, here—. No, Ben, now don't. I'm afeard—."

"I'll give you all of it!"

Tom gave up the brush with reluctance in his face but alacrity in his head. And while the late steamer, Big Missouri, worked and sweated in the sun, the retired artist sat on a barrel in the shade close by, dangling his legs, munched his apple, and planned the slaughter of more innocents. There was no lack of material; boys happened along every little while; they came to jeer, but remained to whitewash. By the time Ben was fagged out, Tom had traded the next chance to Billy Fisher for a kite in good repair; and when he played out, Johnny Miller bought in for a dead rat and a string to swing it with— and so on, and so on, hour after hour. And when the middle of the afternoon came, from being a poor, poverty-stricken boy in the morning, Tom was literally rolling in wealth. He had, beside the things before mentioned, twelve marbles, part of a jew's-harp, a piece of blue bottle-glass to look through, a spool cannon, a key that wouldn't unlock anything, a fragment of chalk, a glass stopper of a decanter, a tin soldier, a couple of tadpoles, six firecrackers, a kitten with one eye, a brass doorknob, a dog collar—but no dog, the handle of a knife, four pieces of orange peel, and a dilapidated old window sash.

He had a nice, good idle time all the while—plenty of company—and the fence had three coats of whitewash on it! If he hadn't run out of whitewash, he would have bankrupted every boy in the village....

The art of persuasion includes meeting people's interests and needs.

---

* * *

Both parties do not always want the same goal for the same reason.

Jack Sprat

Author unknown

Jack Sprat could eat no fat.
His wife could eat no lean.
And so betwixt the two of them,
They licked the platter clean.

Don't assume the other party wants what you want. Find out what each party is interested in. Both of you may be interested in the same thing for different reasons. This will lead to solutions.

---

*   *   *

In his fables, Aesop often refers to methods different parties use to resolve disputes or solve problems.

Aesop's Fables

Retold by Anne Terry White

1. The Mice in Trouble

"It's terrible! Just terrible! We really must do something about it! But what?"

The Mice were talking about the Cat. One by one they were falling into her claws. She would steal up softly on her pussy feet. Then suddenly she would spring—and there was one mouse less.

At last the Mice held a meeting to decide what to do. One said this, another said that. But mostly they spoke about how terrible and sad things were. Nobody had any plan.

Then a young mouse jumped up. "I know what we should do!" he said brightly. "Tie a bell around the Cat's neck! Then we would hear her coming and we would run away fast!"

The Mice clapped their little paws for joy. What a good idea! Why hadn't they thought of it before? And what a very clever little fellow this young mouse was!

But now a very old mouse, who hadn't opened his mouth all this time, got up to speak.

"Friends," he said, "I agree that the plan of the young mouse is very clever indeed. But I should like to ask one question: which of us is going to tie the bell around the Cat's neck?"

The moral is there is no use offering a plan that cannot be carried out.

> *In negotiation, it does not pay to create a solution that cannot be carried out by one or both of the parties.*

2. The Boy and the Nuts

A boy who was very fond of nuts was told one day that he could have a handful.

"As big a handful as I like?" he asked.

"As big a handful as you can take," his mother answered.

The boy at once put his hand into the pitcher of nuts and grasped all his fist would hold. But when he tried to get his hand out, he found he couldn't because the neck of the pitcher was too narrow. He tried and tried to squeeze his hand through. At last he burst into tears. There he stood crying, yet unwilling to let a single nut go.

"The fault is not with the pitcher, my boy," his mother said. "It is your greed that makes you cry. Be satisfied with half as many nuts, and you will be able to get your hand out."

The moral is half a loaf is better than none.

> *In negotiation, you may have to compromise to get something you want and to get a dispute resolved.*

3. The Bundle of Sticks

There was once a man who had four sons. The father loved them very much, but they troubled him greatly. For they were always fighting with one another. Nothing the father said did any good.

"What can I do to show my boys how wrong it is to act this way?" the father thought.

One day he called the boys to him and showed them a bundle of sticks.

"Which of you, my sons, can break this bundle of sticks?" he asked them.

All the boys tried in turn, but not one of them could do it.

Then the father untied the bundle and gave each boy a single stick. "See if you can break that," he said.

Of course, they could easily do it.

"My sons," the father said, "each of you alone is weak. He is as easy to injure as one of these sticks. But if you will be friends and stick together, you will be as strong as the bundle of sticks."

The moral is when people stand together, they are strong.

In negotiation, getting parties to see their mutual interests helps to get a solution.

---

* * *

When people negotiate, they often have hidden interests. This illustration talks about a girl's possible hidden interest when negotiating for the car.

Conclusion

Often negotiation requires creativity both during the process and in creating a settlement.

When parties state their goals, what they say may not be their real goals. Good negotiators find out what the other party really means and ask for clarification.

Negotiation occurred throughout history. Many negotiations require creativity to obtain the truth.

The art of persuasion includes meeting other people's interests and needs.

Good negotiators do not assume the other party wants the same thing they want. Find out what the other party wants. Both parties may be interested in the same thing but for different reasons. A settlement can therefore be reached based on different interests.

Offering a plan of settlement that cannot be carried out is of no use.

In negotiation one may have to compromise to get something one wants and to get a dispute resolved.

In negotiation, getting parties to see their mutual interests helps both to reach a solution.

PART II

Mediation

CHAPTER **7**

The Art of Mediation

After two parties have tried to settle a dispute between themselves but are unable to resolve the conflict, they may seek a third party, a mediator, to intervene. A mediator listens to both parties' views and attempts to effect a reconciliation of the dispute, although in mediation, the parties themselves actually create the agreement. The mediator does not decide on a solution and try to impose it onto the parties. Instead, the mediator facilitates the resolution of the dispute by the parties. Generally, the agreement will be one that meets both parties' needs to some extent.

Mediation has a number of advantages. (1) It is expeditious; rather than waiting to go to court, which may take years, or rather than acting in retaliation or in anger, parties may seek mediation as a quicker method of solving a conflict. (2) It provides time to present a case; mediators often spend more time than a judge is able to spend and can thus examine all the options. (3) Legal representation is not needed; parties do not need legal representation by lawyers, thus lowering the expense of conflict resolution. (4) No court rules apply; because mediation lacks special rules of evidence and court procedures, mediation allows all party views to be addressed. (5) Flexible agreements are created; mediation offers flexibility in creating unique agreements that suit the parties but which may not be available in a court of law.

Mediation, like negotiation, is a process. (See Table 7–1)

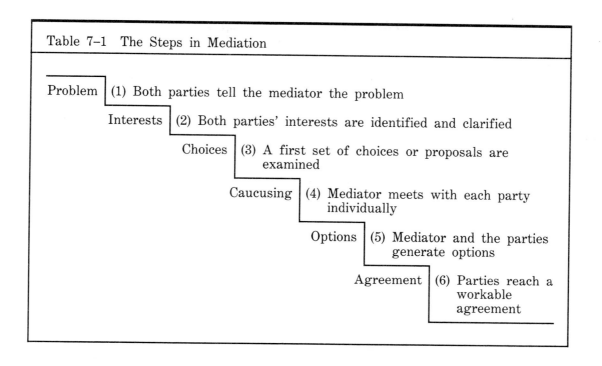

Table 7–1   The Steps in Mediation

Problem | (1) Both parties tell the mediator the problem

Interests | (2) Both parties' interests are identified and clarified

Choices | (3) A first set of choices or proposals are examined

Caucusing | (4) Mediator meets with each party individually

Options | (5) Mediator and the parties generate options

Agreement | (6) Parties reach a workable agreement

The process of mediation requires a third party, a mediator, to intervene between the disputing parties. To accomplish this successfully, the mediator must have special skills and is often specially trained. A skilled mediator is generally: (1) unbiased; (2) an expert listener; (3) respectful; (4) able to get people to work together; (5) able to engender confidence while keeping information confidential. First, the mediator should be a relatively objective individual who has no biases regarding the dispute. Second, the mediator should be someone skilled in listening attentively to the parties, hearing what they are saying and observing what they are feeling. Third, the mediator should treat both parties and their views with respect and concern. Fourth, because the mediator has no authority to impose a solution or agreement, the mediator must be able to help the parties come to an agreement of their own. Last, the mediator must be an individual who can engender the confidence of the parties and who can keep information given during a private caucusing session confidential.

To show how mediation may work in a real situation, let's return to the dispute between John and his father. John wants the car on Saturday night for a date, but his father says no, because he would like to take his wife to the movies. If John and his father are still quarreling,

As mediator, Grandma will not decide the outcome of this dispute but will facilitate John's and his dad's efforts in reaching their own agreement.

John may then want to call in a third person, a mediator, to help solve this problem.

If John were to pick a mediator, he might first think about asking his mother. However, because his mother is the person his father would like to take to the movies, and John may surmise that his mother may want to see the movie with his father, John may ultimately decide not to call in his mother to act as a mediator. For this discussion, let us assume John called his grandmother to mediate the dispute.

John told his grandmother the situation; she agreed to intervene and try to solve the problem. John knows he has not always agreed with his grandmother in the past on certain issues, but he does respect her and trusts that she would try to be fair. She is somewhat objective; she will listen; she will hear both sides; she could help both father and son work out a solution; and she can keep a secret. John also knows his father trusts his grandmother. Therefore, John's grandmother is an appropriate mediator for this dispute.

Table 7–2	
Problem	(1) Both parties tell the mediator the problem

In mediation, both parties must begin by telling the mediator what they see as the problem and their view of the dispute. Often, both parties are very angry at one another because they have already tried negotiating between themselves but have not been able to resolve the conflict. Generally, they come before the mediator with a great deal of anger. This anger may color the way the parties tell their views to the mediator; they may exaggerate or put emphasis on different aspects of the problem. The mediator must make sense of all that is said and try to put the events and statements in a proper perspective.

In John's case, John may angrily tell his grandmother that his father basically does not trust him and is, therefore, refusing to give him the car. He may assert that his father is always trying to get him to study and is using the car as a way of accomplishing this. John's father may tell the grandmother that John is very lazy and has not been trying to do as well as he could in school; thus John does not deserve the car. The grandmother will have to listen to both these views of the problem and put them in a logical perspective. She may determine that the real problem is that they both need the car on the same night at the same time. She may ask them both if that is the real problem and, in all probability, they will agree.

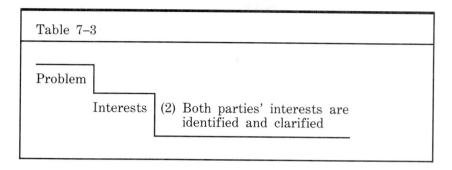

Table 7–3

Problem

Interests | (2) Both parties' interests are identified and clarified

In mediation, like in negotiation, both parties' interests must be identified and clarified. Sometimes these interests go beyond the scope of the apparent dispute. Sometimes these interests are not even apparent to the parties themselves, but they may feel them nonetheless. Therefore, a mediator must not only listen to what is said but must also look behind the words and body language to determine the real interests of the parties.

In John's case, perhaps his father's interest is in maintaining some control over John's actions and in maintaining his role as head of the household. Perhaps John's interest is that of asserting his own growing independence as he matures and that of gaining his father's respect. Certainly both parties are interested in using the car on Saturday night. Grandmother may sense all these interests and feelings and may even want to tell each of the parties about the other's concern. She may tell John that he should be more understanding of his father's concern for John's whereabouts. She may also ask John to try to understand his father's discomfort at having a son who is growing up so fast. Grandmother may tell John's father that he should be more understanding of John's need for more independence and respect. In talking about these interests to both parties, she is giving legitimacy to these interests, and thus, making each party believe his views are being considered. She is also helping them see their problems in a realistic light within the context of normal father/son relationships.

Grandmother, as mediator, should also isolate the individuals' interest: that of getting transportation to their respective events on the same night.

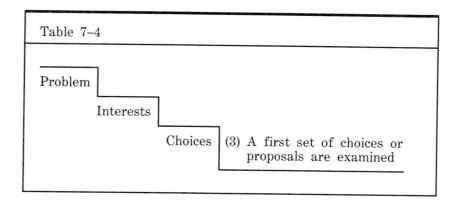

Table 7–4

Problem

Interests

Choices | (3) A first set of choices or proposals are examined

In mediation, after both parties set out their views to the mediator, a first set of choices is examined. These are possible options or alternatives available to the parties for resolving the dispute. These choices may be offered or suggested by the parties themselves or by the mediator. In each case, each choice or **proposal** is weighed against the parties' competing interests and views. The ultimate objective is to find a choice or proposal that meets both parties' needs.

Some of these choices, particularly those suggested by the parties themselves, may be one-sided in that if they were implemented, one party would win and the other party would lose. Because of the parties' anger or hostility, they may suggest choices or proposals that are unreasonable or apparently demanding. The mediator will try to seek a solution wherein both parties will feel they have won something and the dispute no longer plagues them. Though both parties may ultimately have to give up something or compromise, they should be able to walk away from mediation believing that a win-win solution has been attained and a fair result has been achieved.

In John's case, John may first say the right choice or proposal should be one where he gets the car and his father does not; his father may say he should get the car and John should not. John might offer to fill the car with gas or wash the car in exchange for car privileges. John's father may offer to drive John and his date wherever they may want to go. John may ask his father to go to the movies on another night; his father may ask John to change his date.

All these choices or proposals may be offered during the course of the mediation. Ultimately one of these choices may become the final agreement of the parties. Often, because the parties are in conflict, they may not be listening to one another, or they may not be giving serious consideration to the choices mentioned. In this case, let us assume the parties did not agree to any of these proposals. Because of a lack of agreement, grandmother decided to meet individually with John and his father. This step is called **caucusing.**

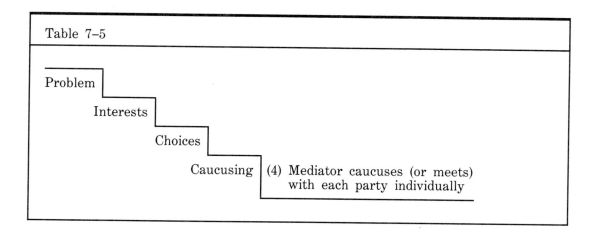

Table 7–5

In mediation, if the parties offer choices or proposals to which none are agreed by the parties, the mediator may want to meet with the parties individually to discuss their views concerning the conflict. This step is called caucusing. During caucusing, the mediator will ask each party probing questions. Sometimes the mediator will try to get some additional facts. Sometimes the mediator will ask "why" to get at the party's underlying interests and concerns. Sometimes the mediator will try to bring the party's expectations in line with reality. Sometimes the mediator will translate and communicate what each side is really saying to one another. The mediator may even try to find out each party's views or explore solutions to which both sides would most likely agree. The mediator may ask questions such as:

"What do you really want to happen?"

"What do you think is the proposal to which both of you most likely would agree?"

"If you were in the other person's shoes, how would you feel?"

"What would you do?"

"What will you do if both of you do not reach an agreement?"

"How much will not agreeing cost you?"

"How would it feel to walk away right now with the whole matter settled satisfactorily?"

"What are some fair ways of settling this problem, fair to you and to them?"

"What if the other party did this, could you do that?"

All these questions will help the mediator get at the parties' real interests and may generate some excellent solutions.

In John's case, when grandmother meets with each party, each may indicate his willingness to settle this whole matter while still wanting to "save face" with the other party. As in this case, when parties often have to live and work together in the future, they will be more likely to try to seek a solution whereby both will feel they have won something but will also feel they can continue to face each other in the future.

During caucusing, all information given to the mediator is kept confidential. The mediator will not reveal this information without permission of the party providing it. The mediator can use the information, however, to guide the parties toward a solution.

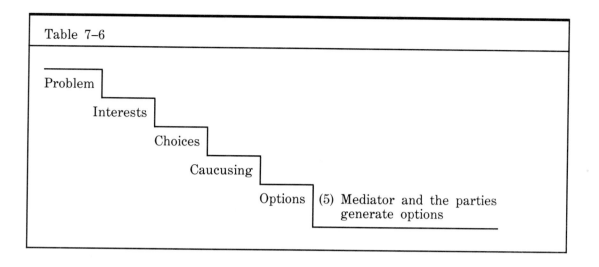

Table 7–6

Problem
    Interests
        Choices
            Caucusing
                Options | (5) Mediator and the parties generate options

In mediation, once the mediator has held a caucus with both parties, the parties and the mediator will then join together to generate some workable options. These options should be such that both parties will win something and will believe a fair result can be achieved. Each option will be considered in light of each party's views and interests as well as its feasibility. The origin of many of these options may be comments and ideas suggested during caucusing.

In John's case, John may suggest to take his father and mother to the movies if they would let him have the car. John's father may now be willing to consider that option and may ask John to do something further, such as pick up his mother from work so that they could all leave early that evening.

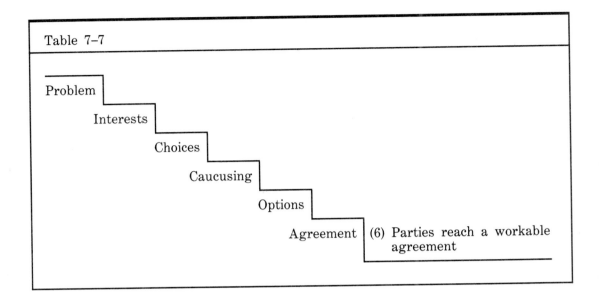

Table 7-7

Problem
    Interests
        Choices
            Caucusing
                Options
                    Agreement | (6) Parties reach a workable
                                    agreement

In mediation, after the parties have discussed all the options and they begin to focus on one that particularly appears to meet both their needs, the mediator should begin to identify this as a possible agreement. However, the agreement must be a workable one in the sense that both parties consider it reasonable, that it is one where both parties are able to accomplish their responsibilities in the context of the agreement, and that some consideration is given as to what might happen if the parties do not carry out the agreement. Sometimes the penalties for not carrying out the agreement become part of the agreement itself along with the chosen option settling the dispute. This agreement is often put in writing or is formalized in some manner.

In John's case, once grandmother has encouraged both John and his father to focus on one reasonable option that they appear to favor, grandmother may repeat the agreement to each of them, receive their promise that they will carry out this agreement, and shake hands to solidify this agreement.

Conclusion

All mediations require identifying the problem, identifying and clarifying interests, examining choices, caucusing, generating options, and reaching a workable agreement.

A mediator's job is not to decide the outcome of the dispute but rather to facilitate the parties' efforts in reaching their own agreement.

A mediator is generally a person who is unbiased, an expert listener, respectful, able to get people to work together, able to engender confidence while keeping information confidential.

Mediation is advantageous because it is fast, it provides time to present the case, no legal representation is required, no court rules apply, and flexible agreements can be created.

Caucusing is a confidential meeting between each party and the mediator.

The parties themselves create the agreement in mediation. The agreement created can be tailored to meet the specific, individual needs of the parties.

Exercises

Try out your mediation skills on the following conflicts. In each case, two students must take the role of each party and a third student must take the role of the mediator. Each party should act as the party in the conflict would and should assert the arguments the party would assert if he or she were before a real mediator. These conflicts can be mediated by one group while the entire class watches and analyzes what is happening. Another procedure might be that the class can be broken into groups of three and all students in the class can try to go through the mediation process using these conflicts.

Conflict 1

A neighbor continues to have loud parties every Saturday and Sunday night, often in the backyard. Much garbage and refuse flies around the neighborhood as a result. The next-door neighbor has continuously complained and has called the police a number of times. This conflict continues to escalate, so both parties have agreed to go to a mediator. One neighbor wants to be able to give parties without the police showing up, and would also like the complaining phone calls to stop. The other neighbor wants quiet on Saturday and Sunday nights, and would also like less garbage on a prized flower garden.

Conflict 2

John pushed Alex in the school hall during class break. Alex got mad and chased John, throwing him against the locker wall. John is convinced Alex stole his math notes the day before the test. Alex says he found them on the floor and there were no names on the pages. Both students share lockers with someone else. John and Alex have never liked one another since last year when they both dated the same girl.

Conflict 3

Acme Corporation has decided to reduce its work force and suspend pay increases to try to make a profit. Stockholders have demanded some action, and as a result, the management of the corporation sees no alternative but to lay workers off and suspend pay increases. Union leaders are angry. They contend the company could make a profit through other alternatives, and they are opposed to any workers losing their jobs. Workers have threatened to strike if this is not resolved by mediation.

Conflict 4 (Real Case)

Read an article in the local newspaper and assign roles to people in class. Try to mediate the dispute.

CHAPTER **8**

Details of the Process

Attributes of a Good Mediator

A mediator has important functions throughout the process of mediation.

First, the mediator's neutrality concerning the parties and the issues is essential. Also, he or she must be nonjudgmental about the parties and issues. Third, the mediator must be a good listener. Further, he or she must indicate fairness and engender the trust of the parties. Last, the mediator must be able to maintain confidentiality. These qualities—neutrality, nonjudgmental attitude, good listening skills, fairness, trustworthiness, and ability to maintain confidentiality—are the primary attributes of a good mediator.

How Mediation Begins

The disputing parties may come to a mediator for a number of reasons: they may believe going to court is too costly given the problem; they may view the problem as getting worse and are frustrated in not being able to resolve it; they may have come to the conclusion that ignoring the other party or, in the alternative, using physical violence does not resolve the conflict; they may not be able to afford an attorney; they may not want to wait a long time for the case to go to court.

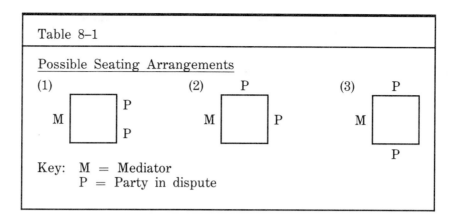

Table 8–1

Possible Seating Arrangements

Key: M = Mediator
       P = Party in dispute

Meeting Place

The parties are generally angry at one another as they enter the room where mediation takes place. In the room there is usually a table with chairs around it.

Where the parties sit in relation to each other and to the mediator may be important. Sometimes when two people sit next to one another, they may be more likely to communicate better and relate to one another. On the other hand, angry and hostile parties might hurt one another if they sit next to one another. If the mediator senses this is so, he or she may ask the parties to sit across the table from one another while the mediator sits in the middle. (See Table 8–1)

Mediator's Opening Statement

A mediator begins by introducing himself or herself and setting the tone of the discussion right at the beginning. The mediator explains the process and the steps of media-

tion, discusses the concept of caucusing, tells each party
the ground rules, and offers that he or she will be asking
questions throughout the mediation process.

Explaining the Process

In discussing the process, the mediator will explain that
mediation is voluntary and that the role of the mediator
is to help both parties reach a solution to their problem
that meets both their needs and is acceptable to both of
them. The mediator may also want to review the advantages of mediation for the parties.

Discussing the Concept of Caucusing

The mediator will discuss the concept of caucusing with
each party individually at some point during the process.
The mediator will explain that during caucusing, only one
party talks to the mediator while the other party leaves
the room. During that time, all information given to the
mediator is strictly confidential and will not be divulged
unless the party agrees.

Telling the Ground Rules

The mediator may want to explain some basic ground
rules. These include: first, that both parties will have an
opportunity to state their views; second, while one person
is talking, the other party cannot interrupt; third, if the
parties reach an agreement, they will abide by the agreement.

The Mediation Session

After the opening statement, the mediator may ask the parties to tell how they see the situation. The parties will discuss the problem, events related to the problem, and other facts. They may even make hostile statements toward one another. To some extent, the mediator must allow the parties to "let off steam." However, the mediator may caution them not to call each other names or use foul language during the discussion.

While both parties tell their views, the mediator will be listening very carefully. The mediator is busy gathering facts, learning about the parties' personalities, determining each party's interests and **priorities** and identifying the express and hidden issues.

The mediator will not act judgmentally or in a biased manner toward either party and will try to view the problem with a neutral tone. The mediator will avoid saying to the parties, "You are right" or "You are wrong." Rather than continue the person-against-person conflict, the mediator will try to refocus or redirect the parties to concentrate on the problem and need for a resolution. Last, the mediator will be thinking about possible plans or solutions to the problem.

After both parties have presented their views, the mediator may begin a brainstorming session by asking the parties to generate a whole range of possible solutions to the problem. The mediator may also ask questions or may have to translate information said by the parties in clearer language. Many times the parties expect too much and are not being realistic about possible solutions to the problem; the mediator may have to put the expectations of the parties in a realistic perspective. The mediator will never place blame on either party. Above all, the mediator will always be looking for a solution that will allow the parties to "save face" and work or live together in the future.

During the course of this discussion, the parties may begin to make offers and counteroffers to one another. The demands of one another may, however, come to a crossroad. At the point where neither party can agree and no resolution is imminent, the mediator may want to caucus with each person individually.

Caucusing

During the caucusing session, one party leaves the room while the other party stays to talk with the mediator. Caucusing serves a number of purposes. First, the mediator may want to get further information that the party may only be willing to say confidentially. All statements made during caucusing are confidential unless the party agrees the information can be divulged. Second, the mediator may want to generate options with the party. Third, the mediator may also want to ask rather tough questions and receive answers the party may not want the other side to hear. Further, during the course of the caucusing session, the mediator may want to remind the party of the not-so-nice alternatives if no resolution to the problem results. The mediator may remind the individual of some problem areas in his or her side of the case and the importance of finding a solution to the problem. For the sake of fairness, both parties are often given caucusing sessions with the mediator.

Closure and Agreement

When the parties and the mediator come together again after caucusing, they work towards **closure** and agreement. The discussion will be directed toward finding the optimal solution that will meet both parties' needs—one that will be realistic and workable, and one with which both parties can agree. This may require modifying or changing options that were previously generated. It may involve coming up with creative solutions not considered before. It may involve compromise on the part of both parties to achieve a resolution to the conflict. Ultimately, it must be the parties themselves that create the solution and implement it.

Carrying Out the Agreement

When an option is discussed where both parties appear to be in agreement, the mediator may redefine it, identify the responsibilities of each party in carrying out the solution, and help the parties work out a timetable for implementing the agreement. The solution, each party's responsibilities, and a timetable for implementation may all be stipulated in the agreement itself.

Conclusion

A mediation begins when negotiations break down but the parties do not want to go to trial.

Given that the parties are embroiled in a dispute, choosing a meeting place and even a seating arrangement is necessary.

The mediator begins with an opening statement explaining the process of mediation, the concept of caucusing, and the ground rules.

The option that is more likely to settle the dispute is one that is workable and realistic to both parties.

The mediation agreement is created by the parties themselves, not the mediator, who only helps the parties reach the agreement. A good agreement sets out the solution, identifies the responsibilities of each party and delineates a timetable for implementing the agreement.

Exercises

Here are two conflicts where the parties have come before a mediator for help. The conflicts are presented as a set of roles for each participant. The teacher will assign you your role, and you may then go through the mediation process.

Conflict 1

Party 1

Your name is Ms. Smith, and you are a tenant in an apartment building. You have two children. For three months, you have asked the landlord to repaint the apartment because the paint is peeling off the walls. You know, however, that your lease contract does not obligate the landlord to repaint the apartment.

While you were in the basement of the building, you found some paint, and one afternoon you and some friends repainted the entire apartment.

When the rent became due at the end of that month, you subtracted $250.00 from the rent, stating to the landlord this was the cost of having your apartment painted. You really got that amount from an estimate you once received from a professional painter.

The landlord has refused to accept the rent check with the reduction for the paint job. He now wants to evict you for failure to pay your full rent. Moving would be costly to you, but you believe that the building has been improved by the painted apartment and that you should get credit for this.

You have not told the landlord that you painted the apartment with his paint.

Party 2

You are Mr. Wilson, the landlord and owner of an apartment building. The building is old and many things constantly break. The repairs are very costly, and you have difficulty paying your mortgage payments to the bank every month. You try to make sure all the apartments are rented by offering a low monthly rental to tenants. However, with the increased repair costs, you cannot afford to offer your tenants too many extras.

One of your tenants, Ms. Smith, has been nagging you to repaint her apartment. You know you are not obligated to repaint it under the lease contract, and you believe that this would be too costly to do so considering first, that her rent is very low, and second, that if you repaint her apartment, all the tenants may want their apartments repainted.

Ms. Smith has given you her rent check this month, with $250 deducted for her cost in repainting the apartment. You will not accept the check, and now you want to evict her for failure to pay this month's rent.

You have seen the apartment, and it does look better. However, you do not want the tenants to think they can get away with deducting money from their rent checks.

Mediator

You are Mr./Ms. Jones, the mediator. Both Mr. Wilson and Ms. Smith have come to you for help in solving their dispute. You have creative problem-solving ability. You are a great listener, and you try to remain neutral whenever you are called in to mediate a dispute. You never place blame on anyone. You pride yourself on the fact that during the last year you have mediated over twenty disputes successfully.

Conflict 2

(Story based on a real dispute as retold by Dean Leonard J. Schrager.)

Party 1

You are Ms. Conklin, president of Conklin Candies, a small family-owned candy-making business. You are proud that you began your candy-making business in your kitchen, and you believe that you produce the freshest and purest candy on the market today.

Your business is small but thriving. You are trying to build it up, but right now you have trouble keeping up with your current orders. You pay your bills month to month.

You package your candies in a decorative candy tin. The tins are specifically designed to fit a certain measured amount of candy. You order these tins from another small company, Tom's Tins. This month you received your usual order of tins and found, to your dismay, that the tin tops were one-half inch too small and the tin bottoms were one-half inch too big. None of the tops matched the bottoms.

This means you will not be able to get your orders out on time. Further, your candy, which contains no preservatives, will get stale and be ruined within three weeks time if not packaged and shipped immediately.

You are desperate. You visualize your whole company folding as a result of this error on the part of the tin company. You have already paid for the tins in advance of the shipment. You have complained to Mr. Tom Taylor, the president of Tom's Tins and he has apologized. He says, however, his company totally relies on only a couple of customers, and he cannot afford to make new tins without being paid for the ones he already made. Further, if new tins are to be made, he would need money in advance to pay for making those tins.

You think you will lose all your candy orders and possibly go bankrupt if this is not straightened out. You cannot afford legal fees, although you would love to take Mr. Taylor to court.

You have decided to go to a mediator.

Party 2

You are Mr. Tom Taylor, president of Tom's Tins, a small tin manufacturing company. You have a small manufacturing business in your garage and are just making ends meet with the couple of tin orders you get every month. You have just a couple of steady tin customers. One major customer is Ms. Conklin of Conklin Candies.

Every month you make candy tins in which she packages her candies. She pays you every month in advance. You use the money to cover the cost of manufacturing the tins.

This month your machines erred and produced tins that were not quite right. Ms. Conklin called you immediately, hysterically screaming that you have ruined her business and that she would sue you. If she did that, you would be out of business. She has already paid you for the tins, and you needed the money to pay for the cost of producing those tins, even though they did not come out right. You cannot afford to remake new tins without getting paid for them.

You realize you will probably go out of business without Ms. Conklin's business, but you have no choice.

You have agreed to go to a mediator.

Mediator

You are Mr./Ms. Jones, the mediator in this dispute. The parties in this dispute have called you in because you have a pretty good business sense and can come up with creative options. You believe this case may go to court if the parties do not come to an agreement. You also believe that because this case involves two small business-es, the costs of going to court will probably ruin both businesses.

You accept the challenge and will proceed with the mediation. You are well known for remaining calm and neutral, engendering the trust of others, maintaining confidentiality, being a good listener, being fair and trustworthy, and helping people come to realistic and workable agreements.

PART III

Arbitration

CHAPTER **9**

The Art of
Arbitration

Arbitration is another tool used to resolve or settle disputes. After disputing parties initially try to settle a conflict between themselves but are unsuccessful, they may call in a mediator to effectuate a resolution. If this fails, however, the parties may agree to appear before an arbitrator who will hear both sides of the dispute. Rather than the parties, it will be the arbitrator who will make the decision. The parties must agree in advance to abide by the arbitrator's decision.

Arbitration is the submission of a dispute by the parties to a disinterested person, an arbitrator, who will make a final judgment. Arbitration may be voluntary (requested by the parties) or compulsory (as in the case where a judge may order arbitration).

In some industries, arbitration is common. For example, during management-labor conflicts, parties are often referred to an arbitrator. Some people have an arbitration clause written into their work contract defining what procedure they should follow if they have a grievance. Many conflicts between nations are brought before an international panel of arbitrators. Sometimes an arbitrator's decision can be appealed in court, but courts give great deference to the arbitrator's decision.

Arbitration differs from mediation. Mediation seeks to compromise the position of the parties and assist them in creating their own agreement that will, for the most part, meet both their needs. Arbitration seeks to leave the decision to a decision maker, the arbitrator. In mediation, the parties themselves create the agreement through the conciliatory efforts of the mediator. In arbitration, the arbitrator decides the outcome of the dispute.

Arbitration is a process of submitting the dispute to a disinterested person, an arbitrator, who will make a final judgment.

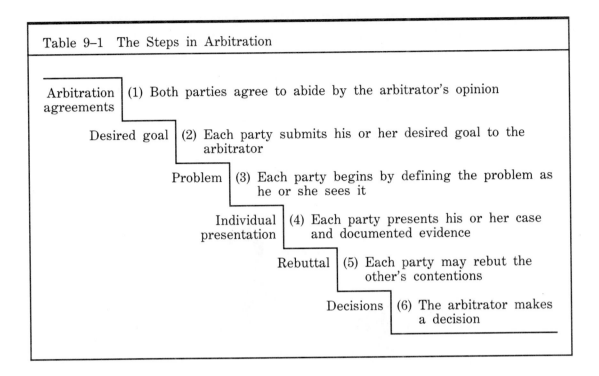

Table 9–1   The Steps in Arbitration

Arbitration agreements — (1) Both parties agree to abide by the arbitrator's opinion

Desired goal — (2) Each party submits his or her desired goal to the arbitrator

Problem — (3) Each party begins by defining the problem as he or she sees it

Individual presentation — (4) Each party presents his or her case and documented evidence

Rebuttal — (5) Each party may rebut the other's contentions

Decisions — (6) The arbitrator makes a decision

Arbitration is a process (See Table 9–1). The process of arbitration requires a third party, an arbitrator, to intervene between the disputing parties, to hear both sides and to make a decision. To accomplish this successfully, the arbitrator is usually highly trained and has special skills. In a philosophical sense, a judge in a bench trial may be viewed as an arbitrator.

Arbitrators have certain special qualities. First, arbitrators must be a disinterested party—they must not know the parties or have any financial or other interest in the outcome of the dispute. If arbitrators have an acquaintance with the parties, they usually recuse, or excuse, themselves from the case. Second, many arbitrators are chosen because they are extremely familiar with the particular subject matter of the case: some are retired executives having been in that particular business; some are professors who teach in that particular field;

some are lawyers having specialized expertise in the field. Third, arbitrators are allowed to examine all available documents. If a defective product is involved in the dispute, they may want to examine the product. Undoubtedly, arbitrators are generally individuals who give both parties the feeling that they will have full opportunity to tell their views of the conflict.

During an arbitration, the parties can be, but do not have to be, represented by attorneys. The reasoning behind this is that rules of evidence and court procedural rules are not applicable to an arbitration. Therefore, the parties themselves do not have to have the specialized knowledge of an attorney to represent themselves and present their case.

Arbitration has a number of advantages. Parties get an opportunity to present their case before a neutral party. The parties are not constrained by rules of evidence and court regulations. Parties are not totally at a loss if they do not win the arbitration; relief may be available in the courts. Arbitration is less costly because neither lawyers nor court time is needed. Generally arbitration is available to the parties sooner than a case could be brought to trial.

To show how arbitration may work in a real situation, let us examine another dispute between John and his father. John wants to stay out past the usually agreed on time of 11:00 P.M. on Saturday night. In this case, John and his father have not been able to resolve this dispute through negotiation between themselves, and further, when grandmother was called in as a mediator, the conflict was still left unresolved.

An arbitrator in this conflict would have to be a totally disinterested party. Let us assume, for the sake of this discussion, Mr. Wilson, a neighbor, was called in to be the arbitrator for the dispute between John and his father. When asked, Mr. Wilson agreed to hear both sides of the dispute and give his decision. Let us also assume, for the sake of this discussion, and generally in arbitration, that both John and his father, like parties in arbitration, have agreed to abide by the decision of Mr. Wilson, the arbitrator.

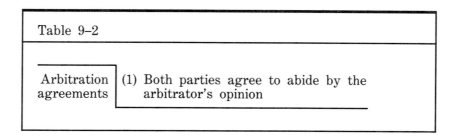

Table 9–2

| Arbitration agreements | (1) Both parties agree to abide by the arbitrator's opinion |

In arbitration, the parties begin by agreeing to abide by the decision of the arbitrator. Generally, under the law, an arbitrator's decision is not binding unless the parties agree that it be binding or if current legislation defines arbitration as binding. Most parties involved in arbitration agree to abide by the arbitrator's decision on the assumption that after they have had their chance to fully present their side of the conflict, the arbitrator will be able to make a fair decision.

In the case of John and his father, both of them have decided that they will abide by the arbitrator's decision.

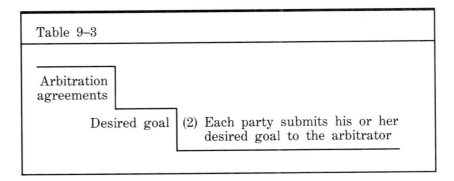

At the outset of arbitration, parties define what they want as a result. In essence, they tell the arbitrator what they would like to see happen. In this way, the arbitrator knows the focus of the decision that must be made as well as the express interests of the parties.

In John's case, John would like to stay out late; his father would like him to return home at 10:30 P.M. They stand, thus far, at a crossroad.

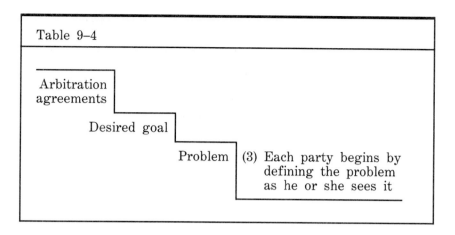

Table 9–4

Arbitration agreements

Desired goal

Problem

(3) Each party begins by defining the problem as he or she sees it

In arbitration, both parties have their chance to tell the arbitrator their views of the problem. In the course of defining the problem, each party may tell the arbitrator extraneous information, may speak to outside issues, may refer to tangentially related incidents, or may cite comments of others. To these, the arbitrator may decide to limit comments to only those he or she believes are pertinent or relevant. Even this limitation, however, is less confining generally than those limitations placed on testimony in a court of law.

In John's case, John may tell Mr. Wilson, the arbitrator, not only that his father has refused to let him stay out late, but may also discuss past occasions wherein John helped his father, did errands, chauffeured his grandmother, and aided his family, thus deserving to stay out late now. He may talk about his father's lack of trust in him and his father's threats of "grounding" him if he does not do better in school. John's father may talk about John's laziness, his poor grades, and his lack of respect for adults. His father may state that he thinks John is untrustworthy. Mr. Wilson, as arbitrator, may limit any or all of the statements by either John or his father as extraneous statements that are not pertinent or relevant to the problem at hand.

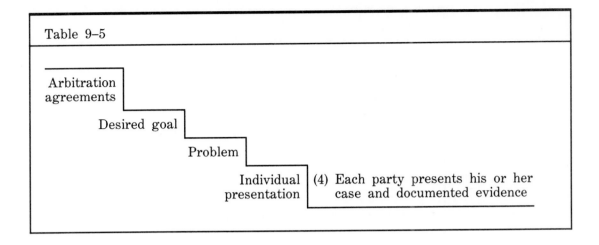

Table 9–5

Arbitration agreements

Desired goal

Problem

Individual presentation

(4) Each party presents his or her case and documented evidence

During the process of arbitration, each party makes a presentation of his or her case. In this presentation, the parties may refer to past relevant incidents leading to the arbitration, they may bring documents related to these past events, and they may even refer to past statements made by others. The only limitations placed on the parties during these presentations is that no party is allowed to interrupt the other party and each party is given an equal opportunity to present his or her views. Both parties should try to focus on the issues, not the people involved.

In the case involving John and his father, both parties will make presentations to Mr. Wilson, the arbitrator. Mr. Wilson may ask each of them questions during the presentation. He may also limit statements that are not relevant or pertinent. Both John and his father should be allowed an equal opportunity to present his case.

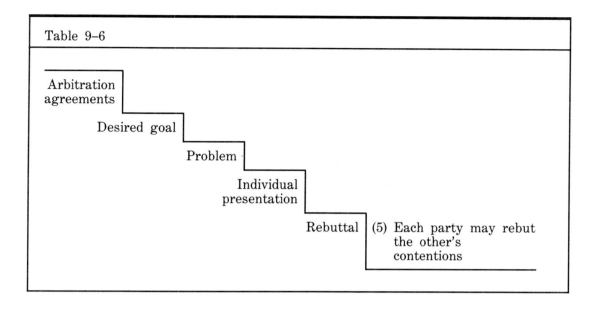

Table 9–6

Arbitration agreements

Desired goal

Problem

Individual presentation

Rebuttal

(5) Each party may rebut the other's contentions

During the arbitration process, after each party has made a presentation of his or her case, each party is then given an opportunity to rebut the other party's contentions. He or she may do so by bringing in further information, showing differing evidence, or indicating contradictory statements. The **rebuttal** gives each party the opportunity to give the arbitrator a different perspective on the issues.

In John's case, both John and his father will be allowed to rebut the other's contentions to Mr. Wilson, the arbitrator.

Table 9–7

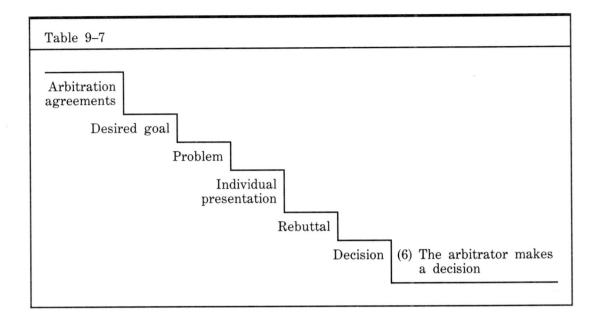

During arbitration, once both parties have had the opportunity to present their side of the case and to rebut the contentions of the other party, the arbitrator may then ask them if they have anything further to add. If the parties answer no, then the time has come for the arbitrator to make a decision. The decision most often is one wherein one party wins and one party loses. Whether a party wins or loses, however, each party has had a fair opportunity to be heard.

John may win this dispute or he may lose it. His father may also win or lose. Each has very little control of the outcome in arbitration, except to the extent that he effectively presents his case.

Conclusion

Arbitration is a process of submitting the dispute to a disinterested person, an arbitrator, who will make a final judgment.

Most arbitration decisions are binding in a court of law.

The arbitration process includes voluntarily agreeing to arbitrate, submitting goals to the arbitrator, defining the problem, presenting each case, rebutting opposing contentions, and decision making by the arbitrator.

An arbitrator is a disinterested person, trained in arbitration, who is chosen for some particular expertise, knowledge, or decision-making ability.

Arbitration is voluntary, and the parties must agree in advance to carry out the arbitrator's decision.

In arbitration, each party presents his or her case, which may include witness statements and other evidence.

After the hearing, the arbitrator makes a decision or agreement on the issues.

Exercises

1. Look in your neighborhood newspaper for examples of arbitrations in your community.

2. Try to find examples of arbitration clauses in contracts. These can often be found in employment contracts, car sales contracts, and purchase agreements. When you do find these, ask yourself why the author of the contract wanted arbitration rather than a trial to settle disputes.

3. Some parties choose arbitration for a number of reasons. Discuss what reasons people might have for choosing arbitration.

   - It is a private process.

   - It is binding on the parties.

   - There is no public record of the proceeding.

   - The rules of evidence and procedure are relaxed.

   - The parties have some input into choosing the arbitrator.

Conflict 1

The management of Acme Corporation has decided not to give pay raises to its employees if it can be proven the employee is not working satisfactorily. Each department in the company has a supervisor who carries out work evaluations. Group #4 has a new supervisor who has given five workers out of twenty an unsatisfactory work evaluation. They will not be getting a raise, though all have been with the company for twenty years and have never received an unsatisfactory rating. The new supervisor says that these employees have never really done a good job but past supervisors have been lax in their evaluations. The new supervisor wants top performance from everyone in the group.

Is arbitration appropriate for this dispute? Why or why not? Is it possible for each of the five cases to be decided differently using arbitration? Why or why not? Does the arbitrator have to decide each case having like facts the same way? Why or why not? What do you think will happen to these cases if they are arbitrated? Try this out in class. Decide what product Acme Company makes and have both a representative from management and an employee argue their sides.

Conflict 2

You have been living with your roommate for four years. You have decided not to live together anymore. You have divided all the things in your apartment except for a television set in an antique cabinet. Both of you paid $50 for the cabinet and split the cost of the television. Both of you want this item. Can you make an argument to an arbitrator why you should get it and the other person should not? Pose your arguments to a chosen classmate who will act as an arbitrator and find out the results. Are there ways to make a creative settlement in this case? Does one person win and one person lose in arbitration? Would the outcome be different if negotiation or mediation were used? Do you think this is a fair process?

CHAPTER **10**

Details of the Process

When parties agree to arbitrate, they have decided to give the decision-making power to a third person, an arbitrator. Many times, arbitration is made part of a contract so that parties in the contract know that if a dispute arises, arbitration is the means by which the dispute will be settled.

A number of organizations around the country provide arbitration services. One famous organization is the American Arbitration Association. Once this organization is notified of a dispute, it will provide the parties with a set of procedures and an impartial arbitrator.

Arbitration Agreement

Initially, the parties must agree to arbitrate. In this agreement, each party agrees to observe the rules and the final agreement. The parties further agree to perform any responsibilities defined by the arbitrator's final agreement.

Selection of an Arbitrator

Once the parties have agreed to arbitration, they will be presented with a list of experienced experts from which one arbitrator will be chosen. Generally, the list is sent to both parties. Each party crosses off objectionable names and numbers the remaining names in order of preference. A mutually agreeable arbitrator is then selected from both lists. Variations of this process are also used. Whatever processes are used to choose the arbitrator, they all have one common element: the parties have input into this choice.

The Hearing

After the arbitrator is appointed, a mutually convenient day and time are chosen. The parties then present their cases before the arbitrator. The arbitrator will then make decisions on the basis of the testimony and evidence presented at the hearing.

First, during the presentation before the arbitrator, the parties take turns defining the problem as they see it. Both will then present their case. Both parties will also submit a statement as to what outcome they would like to occur. At this time, no interruptions can take place except for possible questions by the arbitrator.

During the presentation, documents, witnesses, and testimony can all be presented. These hearings are less formal than court trials, since the rules of evidence or courtroom procedures need not be followed, though in some cases the parties can apply these rules if they wish.

An arbitrator must provide a fair hearing, giving both parties sufficient opportunity to present their respective evidence and arguments. The arbitrator is assumed to be sufficiently knowledgeable in the particular kind of case so as to have technical knowledge and ability to use good judgment. During the arbitration, the parties are allowed to vent their feelings to a great extent even though some of the statements are somewhat irrelevant. The arbitrator will try to keep the testimony within the parameters of the issue and will try not to be influenced by prejudicial or unreliable testimony. All statements and evidence will be taken into consideration by the arbitrator in making the decision.

Rebuttal

After each party has presented his or her case, the other party has an opportunity to rebut statements, documents, testimony, and the general presentation of the opposing side. The parties even have an opportunity to cross-examine opposing witnesses. However, witnesses are rarely present.

Closing Statement

Parties may be given an opportunity to present a closing statement. The arbitrator may ask if the parties have anything further to say or add to the prior presentations. At this time, the parties may want to summarize the testimony and evidence they presented, refute the points made by the opposition, and state the outcome they desire.

The Decision

The arbitrator will then make a decision. Because at the outset of the process, the parties have agreed to abide by the arbitrator's decision, the parties will have to either carry out the decision or appeal the decision to a designated court of law. For the most part, the arbitrator's decision should completely resolve the dispute, and most responsible parties comply with these decisions.

Arbitrators are not required to write opinions explaining the reasons for their decisions, though many times arbitrators do write an opinion and send it to the parties if requested to do so. Everything discussed regarding the cases heard by the arbitrator is strictly confidential and remains so indefinitely.

Conclusion

Arbitration services can be found throughout the country.

The parties must voluntarily agree in advance to arbitrate and abide by the decision of the arbitrator.

Each party participates in choosing the arbitrator who will hear the case.

The time and place of the arbitration is mutually agreed upon.

Both parties are provided an opportunity to present their respective arguments and evidence, including testimony and evidence that ordinarily may not be admissible in a court of law.

After both cases are presented, each party has an opportunity for rebuttal and closing statements.

The arbitrator makes a decision that is generally binding on the parties and will be upheld in a court of law.

Exercises

These conflicts can be presented before an arbitrator for resolution. Some are conflicts you used in studying negotiation and mediation. Discuss the different outcomes of these conflicts when different dispute-resolution techniques are used. Would the outcomes be different, for example, using negotiation and mediation? How would they be different and why?

Conflict 1

Home Steel Corporation has suffered profit losses within the last year due to increased cost of raw materials. As a result, future pay raises will be suspended or 10 percent of the employees will lose jobs. The union leader is angry. He contends that the cost of living has risen and workers need a pay raise. He also contends that no workers should lose jobs. The union leader has threatened a strike unless this is resolved. The company president, Mr. Jones, and the union leader, Mr. Smith, have agreed to take this case before an arbitrator.

Conflict 2

Ms. Richards bought a new Titan automobile at Titan Motor Dealer. Since she purchased the car, she has had nothing but trouble. First the transmission broke, then the brakes, then the paint started peeling, and finally the starter broke. In each case, Ms. Richards brought the car to the dealer for repair. The dealer, Mr. Titan, fixed the car. Now Ms. Richards says the car is broken again and wants the Titan Motor company to buy back the car or give her a new car. She argues that the car is a lemon and she is tired of having it fixed. The dealer says he fixed it, and he will not buy it back. Furthermore, the dealer is concerned that if he buys this car back all customers will want to return the car. The parties have agreed to take this case before an arbitrator.

Glossary

agreement: the act of being in harmony as to a course of action.

arbitration: a hearing and determination of a case by a person chosen by the parties or appointed; it can be voluntary or compulsory.

arbitrator: a person chosen or assigned to hear a case and make a determination.

caucusing: in mediation, where mediator talks privately with one of the parties.

closure: the act of coming to an end by both parties.

conflict: a disagreement of ideas, interests, or principles between people or groups.

dispute: a controversy, debate, argument, or quarrel.

goal: the end toward which effort is directed.

interest: a party's concern.

mediation: intervention by a third person between conflicting parties to help facilitate a resolution and create their own agreement.

mediator: an intervening person who helps disputing parties work out their own solution.

negotiation: the process of conferring with another individual to resolve a problem.

negotiator: one who uses the process of negotiation; this could be a person negotiating on his or her own behalf or someone who represents that person, such as a lawyer.

obstacle: something that stands in the way of successful resolution.

option: a possible choice or alternative for action.

party: a person, an individual, a group, an institution, or an entity involved in a conflict.

plan: a method or procedure devised for doing something or achieving a goal.

priority: ranking things in order of importance or requiring attention.

problem: a question raised for consideration or solution.

proposal: an offer for consideration.

rebuttal: a contradiction, disproval, or response to what was already said.

Bibliography

Alternative Dispute Resolution

Cook, Roehl, and Sheppard, *Neighborhood Justice Centers Field Test*, U.S. Department of Justice, National Institute of Justice, February (1980).

Freedman and Ray, *State Legislation on Dispute Resolution*, American Bar Association, Washington, D.C., June (1982).

Johnson, Jr., Kantor, and Schwartz, *Outside the Courts: A Survey of Diversion Alternatives in Civil Cases*, National Center for States Courts, January (1977).

The Justice System Journal, *Alternative Dispute Resolution*, West Publishing Co., St. Paul, Minn., vol. 9/2, Summer (1984).

Marks, Johnson, Jr., and Szanton, *Dispute Resolution in America: Processes in Evolution*, National Institute for Dispute Resolution, (1984).

McGillis and Mullen, *Neighborhood Justice Centers, An Analysis of Potential Models*, National Institute of Law Enforcement and Criminal Justice, U.S. Department of Justice, October (1977).

155

Ray, *Alternative Dispute Resolution: Bane or Boon to Attorneys?* The Special Committee on Alternative Means of Dispute Resolution of the Public Services Activities Division, American Bar Association, Washington, D.C., (1982).

Sander, *National Conference on Minor Disputes Resolution,* American Bar Association, Washington, D.C., May (1977).

Sander and Snyder, *Alternative Methods of Dispute Settlement—A Selected Bibliography,* ABA Committee on Resolution of Minor Disputes, Division of Public Services Activities, American Bar Association, Washington, D.C., December (1979).

Shaffer, *Legal Interviewing and Counseling in a Nutshell,* West Publishing Co., St. Paul, Minn. (1976).

Negotiation

Bellow and Moulton, *The Lawyering Process: Negotiation,* The Foundation Press, Inc., Mineola, N.Y. (1981).

Cohen, *You Can Negotiate Anything,* Lyle Stuart, Inc., Secacus, N.J. (1980).

Fisher and Ury, *Getting to Yes,* Penguin Books, Ltd., New York, N.Y. (1981).

Illinois Institute for Continuing Legal Education, *Attorney's Guide to Negotiations,* (1979).

Jacker, *Effective Negotiation Techniques for Lawyers,* The National Institute for Trial Advocacy (1981).

Mediation

Ray, *Alternative Dispute Resolution: Mediation and the Law, Will Reason Prevail?* The Special Committee on

Dispute Resolution of the Public Services Division, American Bar Association, Washington, D.C., (1983).

Ray, *Alternative Dispute Resolution: Who's in Charge of Mediation?* The Special Committee on Alternative Means of Dispute Resolution of the Public Services Activities Division, American Bar Association, Washington, D.C., (1982).

Volpe, Christian, and Kowalewski, *Mediation in the Justice System*, The Special Committee on Dispute Resolution of the Public Services Division, American Bar Association, Washington, D.C., (1982).

Arbitration

AAA General Counsel's Annual Report, *Arbitration and the Law, 1983*, American Arbitration Association (1983).

Coulson, *Business Arbitration—What You Need to Know*, 2d ed., American Arbitration Association, New York, N.Y. (1982).

Elkouri and Elkouri, *How Arbitration Works*, 3d ed., The Bureau of National Affairs, Inc., Washington, D.C. (1974).

Gold and Mackenzie, *Wide World of Arbitration, An Anthology*, American Arbitration Association, New York, N.Y. (1978).

Goldberg, *A Lawyer's Guide to Commercial Arbitration*, American Law Institute, American Bar Association, Philadelphia, Penn. (1977).

Nolan, *Labor Arbitration Law and Practice in a Nutshell*, West Publishing Co., St. Paul, Minn. (1979).

Widiss, *Arbitration, Commercial Disputes, Insurance, and Tort Claims*, Practicing Law Institute, New York, N.Y. (1979).

Literature

Edwin, ed., *The Works of Plato*, The Modern Library, Simon and Schuster, Inc., New York, N.Y. (1956).

Maxwell, *The Bible Story*, Review and Herald Publishing Association, Washington, D.C. (1955).

Moffitt, *Tales from Ancient Greece*, Silver Burdett Company, Morristown, N.J. (1979).

Montgomery, *Listening Made Easy*, Amacom, New York, N.Y. (1979).

Retold by Anne Terry White, *Aesop's Fables*, Random House, New York, N.Y. (1964).

Twain, *The Adventures of Tom Sawyer*, The John C. Winston Co., Philadelphia, Penn. (1957).